Juni Felix has created a life-changing book by sharing practical guidance for emotional healing. With this groundbreaking work, readers can take tiny steps to open the door to personal transformation. If you need more hope in your life (and who doesn't?), I urge you to let Juni's book be your guide.

B. J. FOGG, PhD, behavior scientist and director of Stanford University's Behavior Design Lab

I love the Tiny Habits method and use it in our work every day. This is a powerful book that can change your life quickly and permanently. Juni Felix is a wonderful guide to help you move toward an abundant life.

DANIEL G. AMEN, MD, founder of Amen Clinics and author of *Your Brain Is Always Listening*

When you meet Juni, she just loves on you with joy and honesty. Then you read this book and you understand where it comes from. It's from her life to help you in your life. It's real, and it's through the lens of God's Word. Good combo.

BEN CALHOUN, friend and lead singer of Citizen Way

WITHDRAWN

YOU ARE WORTH THE WORK

THE WORK

Moving Forward from Trauma to Faith

JUNI FELIX

A NavPress resource published in alliance
with Tyndale House Publishers

NavPress is the publishing ministry of The Navigators, an international Christian organization and leader in personal spiritual development. NavPress is committed to helping people grow spiritually and enjoy lives of meaning and hope through personal and group resources that are biblically rooted, culturally relevant, and highly practical.

For more information, visit NavPress.com.

You Are Worth the Work: Moving Forward from Trauma to Faith

Copyright © 2021 by Juni Felix. All rights reserved.

A NavPress resource published in alliance with Tyndale House Publishers

NavPress and the NavPress logo are registered trademarks of NavPress, The Navigators, Colorado Springs, CO. *Tyndale* is a registered trademark of Tyndale House Ministries. Absence of ® in connection with marks of NavPress or other parties does not indicate an absence of registration of those marks.

The Team:
David Zimmerman, Acquisitions Editor; Heather Maryse Campbell, Copy Editor; Sarah K. Johnson, Proofreader; Olivia Eldredge, Operations Manager; Ron C. Kaufmann, Designer

Cover photograph of paper butterfly copyright © matju78/Depositphotos. All rights reserved.

Cover illustration of circuit board copyright © tom19275/Depositphotos. All rights reserved.

Author photo by Juni Felix, copyright © 2021. All rights reserved.

All Scripture quotations, unless otherwise indicated, are taken from the Holy Bible, *New International Version,*® *NIV.*® Copyright © 1973, 1978, 1984, 2011 by Biblica, Inc.® Used by permission. All rights reserved worldwide. Scripture quotations marked CEB are taken from the Common English Bible, copyright © 2011. Used by permission. All rights reserved. Scripture quotations marked ESV are from The ESV® Bible (The Holy Bible, English Standard Version®), copyright © 2001 by Crossway, a publishing ministry of Good News Publishers. Used by permission. All rights reserved. Scripture quotations marked MSG are taken from *The Message*, copyright © 1993, 2002, 2018 by Eugene H. Peterson. Used by permission of NavPress. All rights reserved. Represented by Tyndale House Publishers. Scripture quotations marked NKJV are taken from the New King James Version,® copyright © 1982 by Thomas Nelson. Used by permission. All rights reserved. Scripture quotations marked NLT are taken from the *Holy Bible*, New Living Translation, copyright © 1996, 2004, 2015 by Tyndale House Foundation. Used by permission of Tyndale House Publishers, Carol Stream, Illinois 60188. All rights reserved.

Some of the anecdotal illustrations in this book are true to life and are included with the permission of the persons involved. All other illustrations are composites of real situations, and any resemblance to people living or dead is purely coincidental.

For information about special discounts for bulk purchases, please contact Tyndale House Publishers at csresponse@tyndale.com, or call 1-855-277-9400.

ISBN 978-1-64158-264-3

Printed in the United States of America

33614082410019

27	26	25	24	23	22	21
7	6	5	4	3	2	1

Dedicated with love to all my fellow mutants, misfits, and ragamuffins.

CONTENTS

Introduction

THE HEARTACHE you woke up with this morning, that pain in your soul that makes even the task of receiving hope for the new day exhausting—that heartache is not who you are. The abuses, losses, and betrayals you've experienced do not have to continue to cast a dark shadow over your life. Your journey is not over, and you are never alone. Your situation is not your destiny, and sorrow isn't your permanent address.

Contrary to what many have taught and believed for too long, trauma recovery has nothing to do with praying all the right prayers and doing all the right things. Complex trauma affects every part of your body, mind, soul, and spirit.

This is why for most of us, praying a prayer, walking an aisle, or even making a heartfelt profession of faith is simply not enough. Soul-care is essential, and though God can bring order to any chaos and healing to every broken place, you and I must be wise, determined, focused, and willing to partner with Him every day if we want to move forward.

Recovery has very little to do with the amount of faith you have; it has everything to do with your acceptance of and commitment to a lifelong healing journey.

I'm so sorry for what you've been through. It wasn't fair. It wasn't right, and you didn't deserve it. You will never forget what it feels like to suffer so much—but you can be well. You can find peace and everyday rest for your soul.

Your recovery from deeply personal trauma is possible, and it unravels in the same way it was created: one decision after the next, accumulating into your present reality.

Please Stop Blaming Yourself

If you feel stuck in your sadness and sorrow, after nearly a lifetime of experience, I know it's an extremely hard way to live.

Perhaps (like me) you're a trauma survivor who is proactive and committed to fighting hard for wellness. You take your mental health seriously, reading articles, attending workshops and conferences. You set well-thought-out goals and work hard to make progress and to heal from the abusive scenarios that left you wounded.

Yet still you struggle to manage your symptoms and responses to the daily triggers that send you spiraling into discouragement, self-condemnation, and depression.

I want you to know that the cycle of trying, failing, and blaming yourself can end today, because human behavior is not random or unpredictable—it's systematic. Once you understand how human behavior actually works, you can design systems that will keep you moving forward for good.

The key to breakthrough is found when we learn how to scale down our behaviors and convert to a mindset and lifestyle of continual TinyHabits that move us toward good.

We were lovingly designed to grow and move forward through small, one-at-a-time baby steps. This is why we start life as tiny, helpless babies: Love from God is experienced incrementally and expressed as we grow.

Our culturally conditioned mindset of "go big or go home" has caused us to continually feel bad about ourselves for not achieving these big goals.

Behavior Design proves that long-term, sustained change for good is accomplished only by feeling good, not bad. We don't change for good when we feel condemned or ashamed.

So please stop blaming yourself. It's not a personal or moral failing—you need only to understand the system that God created and demonstrated thousands of years ago.

Because of the way your mind was designed, you've been gifted with the ability to rise above and move forward from any and every kind of trauma to faith and—if you really want it—to joy.

Say the Word *Quest* Out Loud

Recovery is a lot like embarking on a quest. It's often difficult, and it requires courage like you've never known. It's never about simply "getting over it."

For many of us, parts of our stories are impossible to get over. You will never forget what you've been through, but you can move forward. It can be well with your soul.

A quest is an arduous journey filled with obstacles and opportunities that can only be completed one resolute step after the next. There will be battles fought, lost, and won. Times of rest and renewal will be mixed up with celebrations and ceremonies, birthdays and funerals. You will see times of faithfulness and disappointment swirled up with the mundane and the miraculous, all working together for you.

Many of us are born into a culture and a mindset that idolize health, wealth, and celebrity; and we join the chase in the unrelenting pursuit of happiness. Yet those of us who are trauma survivors struggle. We are often stumbling, staggering, and limping along as we try to keep up with the frenzied pursuit of this toxic abstraction that's always on the move.

We think we don't have time to invest in ourselves so that we can receive the healing gifts of peace, soul rest, and joy that are God's gifts to us through faith.

This book will help you stop the exhausting pursuit of happiness that always fades, and instead to begin an adventurous, joy-producing quest where each tiny step will lead you closer and closer to a life of fulfilling faith—the kind of faith that allows you to recover from and transcend anything this troubled world brings your way.

Because of the transcendent power of true joy, no matter what challenges and heartaches you face in your healing journey, as a person committed to true wellness, with an identity rooted in love, you will overcome. And your life will become a beacon of light that helps others find their way home.

When it comes to designing a life that isn't controlled by grief and sorrow, you'll have to do some things that are different—things that feel weird and uncomfortable at first. That takes courage.

Reading this introduction is a tiny, victorious choice and a sure step in the right direction. I pray you'll take the next. Together we can move forward in what I call the *quest for joy*. Like all quests, it begins with one tiny step. You can begin right now by simply saying the word *quest* out loud. As one of my favorite authors wrote, "It is an extraordinary word, isn't it? So small and yet so full of wonder, so full of hope."[1]

TinyHabits Keep You Moving Forward

As an expert Behavior Design teacher, I feel honored to have this opportunity to share with you one of the greatest blessings of wisdom I've ever encountered. The concepts, models, and methods you'll learn about are part of a personal treasury of more than twenty-five years of prayer, research, and practice.

Created by Dr. B. J. Fogg, a behavior scientist at Stanford University, Behavior Design is a comprehensive system for thinking clearly about human behavior and designing simple ways to transform lives.

This is a guidebook filled with TinyHabits, based on how human behavior and psychology actually work. If you are consistent in using these simple tools throughout your day, you'll soon discover how easy it is to weave hundreds of tiny—but mighty—moments of victory, encouragement, and celebration into your life.

When I write the compound word *TinyHabit* in this book, I don't mean that the habit itself is tiny (even though it often is).

I'm referring to behavior change using B. J. Fogg's innovative TinyHabits® method. I'm grateful to Dr. Fogg for what this method has meant in my life, and I believe it will help you as well!

Recovery quests are long and winding, like a multilevel role-playing game or the *Lord of the Rings* trilogy. Embarking on one takes much more than stumbling upon some doorway and simply walking through it. In order to make it to the other side of your sorrow, heartache, and regret, you'll have to armor up, train hard, learn your gifts, trust your allies, and do the work. But if you're unwilling, I'm sorry—you're not going to make it. And I really want you to make it. That's why I came back for you.

So if you're ready and you're willing, let's go. I'll show you the way.

Chapter 1

YOU ARE WORTH DOING THE WORK

Life beyond Monstrous Things

"Why is light given to those in misery,
and life to the bitter of soul,
to those who long for death that does not come,
who search for it more than for hidden treasure,
who are filled with gladness
and rejoice when they reach the grave?
Why is life given to a man
whose way is hidden,
whom God has hedged in?
For sighing has become my daily food;
my groans pour out like water.
What I feared has come upon me;
what I dreaded has happened to me.
I have no peace, no quietness;
I have no rest, but only turmoil."

MY MOTHER'S PRAYER (JOB 3:20-26)

WHEN SHE FINALLY DIED, suddenly there was all this space in my life. My mother was severely mentally ill, with multiple diagnoses, for as long as I can remember. Orphaned in Tokyo at age four, she was never well enough to consistently care for my six siblings and me. As the second oldest, I spent most of my childhood on suicide watch, hoping every day that she wouldn't take her own life.

Every single day was a struggle. Every conversation and encounter offered uncertainty, tension, and—all too often—deep heartache.

Then, all at once, she was gone, and the anticipation of these familiar feelings burned away, leaving vast, empty spaces. Sad and overwhelmed by sorrow for as long as I knew her, the only aspiration she ever expressed was that she wanted to die. This became her legacy.

At some definitive moment in her life, she'd achieved and mastered a state of mind where sadness was no longer a feeling—it was her identity. It was what she believed was most true about herself.

For as long as I can remember, I did everything I could to help her see that regardless of what she was feeling, there was always hope. In many ways, though I know better, I still wonder deep within if I failed her. Maybe I was one conversation too early or too late. If you've ever been on suicide watch, you know exactly what I'm describing here.

Consequently, my journey requires acceptance and acknowledgment of the ongoing battle against the darkness I was born into. Despite all the confusion, abuse, hunger, and homelessness I experienced as a child, somehow I knew there had to be another way.

Throughout my growing years, many kind people made time

to help me navigate the labyrinth of my life. I started trauma therapy when I was only four years old. I may never know who suggested that I begin professional treatment so early, but I will always be grateful. I am living proof that the right care, determination, wisdom, and guidance make all the difference. Your life can show this too.

I spent my growing-up years trying to make sense of the chaos. I worked as hard as I could to manage my sorrow. By the time I was a teenager, I'd developed the habit of researching, studying, collecting, and testing every bit of information I could find about the human mind and recovery. I knew that there had to be something that would enable me to successfully navigate the nearly constant flow of reminders of my chaotic and pain-filled childhood. I also knew that I didn't want to become like my mother: a continual source of pain, frustration, and disappointment to herself and others.

I committed to doing everything I could to maintain my sanity and figure out how to actually live and not just survive.

There are few things as debilitating as unresolved sadness. When we are drifting around in our sad seasons, it's easy to believe the lie that something deep within us is irreparably broken. The feelings of fear, anger, and regret seem to overwhelm and consume us, and it's very difficult to imagine a way out.

Sadness left unchecked and unexplored leads to a state of pervasive sorrow. Once you've arrived at sorrow, everyday life becomes a chore and even the thought of getting out of bed can take everything you've got. Before you know it, you've chosen an identity sculpted by your sadness.

The Labyrinth

One of my favorite movies as a child was *Labyrinth*. It's the story of a teenage girl named Sarah who thinks she's pretending when she casts a spell and sends her baby brother to a land filled with goblins, warlocks, and other monstrous things.

The lonely Goblin King has been watching her and waiting for a chance to bring her to his world and keep her as his prisoner forever.

After she casts the spell, he appears to her and explains that she must solve the labyrinth if she wants to bring her brother home. His hope, of course, is that she will fail, just like all the others before her, so that he might keep her and her brother as his prizes in the chaotic, fear-filled, dangerous land he rules.

Maybe, like me, you grew up in a land of monstrous things. It was mostly dark, scary, confusing, and heartbreaking. You worried at times when you heard footsteps in the dark.

You may have suffered emotional, physical, sexual, or spiritual abuse. Like background music playing 24/7 in your mind, the sadness threatens to consume you. One wrong move and the dam might break, allowing heartache to come rushing over you like a tsunami. So you're always on alert, and you're constantly tired from holding it all inside.

The Psychological Fun House Mirror Maze

Maybe you've been to a mirror maze at a carnival or state fair. Every mirror reflects back at you, but the images are distorted in various ways: Your head is stretched wide, or your torso is stretched long and thin, or your features are ballooned out. You may even crash into a wall that seems to be a passageway.

Living with unrecovered trauma can be like this: Everything is distorted, confusing, hope depleting, and *just wrong*. You don't even know how you know it's wrong—you just know. I call this experience the *psychological fun house mirror maze*.

The entrances to these kinds of inner locations vary. Some people, like me, are born into the labyrinth. Others wander in because they can't let go of great losses in their lives. Or maybe someone led them there when they were too young to know any better. They trusted the wrong people, and by the time they realized this, it was too late and they'd lost their way. Maybe this is you. You have lost yourself. You no longer know how to live—you only know how to survive. No matter how you came to this place of sadness, once you arrive, you're branded in your soul with sorrow. As the years pass, you spend every minute of the day just trying to make it through. Sometimes you search for the way out, hoping to arrive in a place where you may never have been but you know exists: *a place of love, peace, safety, and even joy*.

The Most Important Decision

One of life's greatest mysteries is that every one of us knows there's a place eternally filled with hope, safety, rest, beauty, and joy. The longing for this place silently mocks the person trapped in their sorrow.

I felt trapped by that sorrow for most of my growing-up years, though I'd always been the family optimist who made it her responsibility to remind everyone that no matter what happened, things would somehow work out for good and we'd all be okay.

Thankfully, in the midst of the chaos, I made the first part of a decision that made all the difference for my future.

When I was twelve, I was taken to Dachau, one of the largest death camps in Germany. I'm not sure whose bright idea it was to take a school bus filled with children to a concentration camp for a field trip, but there I was.

As we walked through the abandoned gas chambers and viewed the horrific incineration ovens, I felt the tangible presence of evil for the first time.

By then I already knew that life was very hard and often heart-breaking, but I had no idea that humans could be so utterly evil.

Right there, I made a decision: *There's enough abuse. Enough sorrow. Enough hunger. Enough evil, and enough suffering. I don't know how, but I will be a part of the good in this world.* I promised this to myself because I didn't know if anyone else was listening or even cared.

Fast forward to eleventh grade. I had to help take care of my family, so for half the day I went to high school, and during the other half I worked as a data-entry clerk at an insurance company. There I met a kind woman, Mrs. Linda Jarvis, who offered me my first Bible for teens.

She didn't pressure or preach. She just gave it to me and said that it might help me understand the truth about my worth. At that time, I sincerely believed I had absolutely no worth and that if there was a god, he was uncaring, unfair, abusive, and unavailable when I needed him the most.

The more I read the Scriptures, the more I discovered that I was wrong about so many things.

Through those pages, I learned about the most kind, compassionate, good, and joyful person I'd ever heard of: *Jesus*. And as I got to know Him, I met God.[1] Jesus gave me faith to believe and offered me the chance to see that there was indeed an altogether different way to live: the way of love, gratitude, peace, and joy. Most importantly, He taught me how to pray.

It was then that I made the second part of my decision—and it fit quite nicely with the first. I decided, *I will be a part of the good in this world by doing all I can to live and love like Jesus.*

And so began my quest to try to reconcile what I knew and experienced about the reality of abuse and evil in this world with the existence of an all-powerful, all-knowing, loving God.

It's All So Unfair

In the Bible, there's a verse from the Psalms that beautifully describes the beginning of a journey marred by sorrow: "Behold, I was brought forth in iniquity, and in sin did my mother conceive me."[2]

Iniquity is a word that refers to immoral or grossly unfair behavior. It's the perfect way to describe how it feels to be born into a whirlwind of traumatizing experiences—events that culminate in decades of life wounded, stunted, and scarred by chaos, abuse, poverty, sadness, and loss.

It's all so unfair—but it's not the end of your story. Your life did not end the moment the abuse and trauma began. Your story goes on, continues, and then ends like all the others—with one tiny decision after the next, as you design the life you believe you most deserve.

The choice I'm offering you right now can make all the difference for the rest of your life. If you want to be well, it's the most important commitment you can make.

It's simply this: *Will you accept your lifelong healing journey?*

This decision means you are ready and willing to consider new ways of thinking. New ideas and methods for designing new habits will continually empower you to keep moving forward toward the good and prosperous life God planned and wants for you.

Relationship Status: It's Complicated

Healing from deep emotional pain is not like the process of healing from physical pain. From diagnosis to remedy, when it comes to illness or injury, there's typically some sort of logical treatment plan. It starts with the doctors and nurses—your first allies in recovery—and often moves to prescriptions, specific instructions, and an estimated timeline. These elements subtly and continually produce hope for relief and recovery.

But the pain caused by personal, complex trauma is much more complicated. It drills down deep into every part of your being, and it's nearly impossible to design a sequential, linear plan for recovery.

The unique negative manifestations of the physical, mental, emotional, and spiritual disorders caused by trauma are often surprising. Unexpected manifestations of unresolved pain can cause setbacks even after significant progress has been made.

For example, trauma caused by abuse from a parent or caretaker complicates every human relationship in your life—socially, professionally, and personally—because it so deeply wounds your ability to trust. You may not even trust yourself and your ability to discern what's real or who is safe.

Depending on how early the trauma and abuse began, your brain will continually bathe itself in stress response hormones—especially if the abuse began before you could speak, as some of mine did.

The psychological term for this is *preverbal trauma*. Its effects linger well into the grown-up years, as survivors struggle to understand and mitigate what we've experienced during a time in which we literally had no words to describe what was happening to us.

In addition to the psychological damage, your relationship with your body is also complicated by continual fight, flight, or freeze reactions that you're constantly trying to understand, soothe, and survive.

This is why commitment to your healing journey is so important.

Throughout the course of your day, you may be continually exposed to tiny reminders created by the original trauma. These reminders are commonly called *triggers*, and they serve as prompts—like notifications on your phone. They tell your mind that you must take specific action immediately to manage the pain.

You may either respond or ignore—and each of these behaviors creates specific outcomes.

Triggers are wounded spots in our damaged souls, and when something touches them, the pain rises up immediately. Triggers are subtle, and their sources lie deep within the subconscious mind. Until something activates them, they remain hidden. It might be a song, a scent, a person, or even the way a room is laid out.

Because of this, you may struggle to cope with the effects of experiences that wounded you deeply. The moments when these triggers and prompts cause you to stumble can be very discouraging.

The exhaustion caused by not understanding and managing them can negatively impact every relationship you have because they can cause you to feel out of control. And "it's impossible to get close to someone who is always trying to be in control."[3]

Your decision to commit to your healing journey opens the door for you to find the right tools, such as the TinyHabits you'll learn about in this book. Creating and practicing TinyHabits will enable you to respond to your triggers in healthy, wise, and compassionate ways.

In time, you'll see how your triggers will become healthy reminders of how powerful you are, and they will allow you to proactively overcome, grow stronger, and succeed.

The Message of Sorrow

Once I understood the superpower of TinyHabits for continual victory in every area of life, it was a breakthrough that helped me see how I could move from any feeling of sorrow to celebration, then peace, and then joy.

You now have access to this wisdom as well.

The next step in the process is to slow down and listen to the messages your sorrow is trying to communicate to you. Think of it this way: If someone you care about is crying, the first thing you'll probably ask them is "What happened? What's wrong?" And then you'll listen to see if you may be able to help them recover.

Your sorrow is sending you a loving reminder to slow down, stop, and acknowledge and answer these questions.

Sorrow is a gift.[4] It's a signal to slow down and stop running for your life, because *you can never outrun your sorrow*. It always catches up with you and eventually takes you down.

Sorrow is an invitation to stop and recover. It's the chance you're given to finally see that the ways you're choosing to numb your pain are harming you and the people you love.

Your sorrow is trying to tell you that though the trauma that created it was not your fault, recovery needs to become your new full-time objective, because ignoring this responsibility is costing you your life.

Trauma Is Bad Code

Though I began trauma therapy at age four, I can only vividly remember my sessions from around age nine. Thankfully, that's not the only memorable thing that started in my life that year. That was the year I fell in love with the Apple IIe computer at school. The moment I pressed the power button and began loading up my digital wagon to conquer the quest of the Oregon Trail, I fell in love with the way things work: the entire concept of inputs, outputs, systems design, models, methods, creative communication and collaboration, and coding—the works! I took my first computer programming class in tenth grade simply because the earlier grades didn't offer the elective. Among other things, basic computer programming helped me understand the grand design and gift of our amazing human minds.

In coding and systems design, every keystroke, space, and symbol that makes up each line of code is necessary for the program to run efficiently and expertly. Research reveals that our minds, emotions, and nervous systems communicate, collaborate, and process information in similar and sometimes in exactly the same ways as the programs that run our technology.

Trauma is bad code. It infects your entire system and causes multiple processes to go wrong. In order to function and survive, your mind has created strings of thoughts and responses made up of countless tiny components.

Your negative thoughts directly generate the emotions that lead to the behaviors and habits that run like a bad program along familiar paths, generated by thousands of triggers embedded in your everyday life. And you're tired—worn out by sadness and even by the idea of receiving hope for the new day.

My ongoing studies in the psychology of systems design and coding eventually opened the door for me to learn directly from and collaborate with one of my favorite professors: Dr. B. J. Fogg, a behavior scientist at Stanford University.

Quite some time ago, beginning with persuasive technology way back before anyone believed computers could be persuasive, Dr. Fogg discovered what I believe to be an $E=mc^2$-equivalent theory and formula for human behavior. His theory revealed that human behavior is not random, and it's not unpredictable—it's systematic. Once you understand the system, you can design strategies for desired behaviors, outcomes, and aspirations that work for good.

This is why I teach Behavior Design—I know these systems, models, and methods work. They are used for innovative digital tools, such as Instagram, as well as in thousands of good products, helpful systems, and useful services enjoyed every day all over the world.

Your decision to make tiny yet transformative choices is exactly like determining the individual keystrokes that make up the lines of good code. These TinyHabits will keep you moving forward toward wellness every single day.

With consistent practice using TinyHabits, you'll soon become a master at creating a stream of Tiny Celebrations right when you need them to empower the next good step in your healing journey.

You Are Worth Doing the Work

Perhaps your sorrow is not because of something lost but because of something that was stolen. You are a trauma survivor—even on your best days, you know your heart is still shattered. I've been there too.

I believe that sorrow is a gift from God that helps us do much more than just survive. Jesus was described as "a man of sorrows, acquainted with deepest grief."[5]

The gift of sorrow is what fuels His passion and ongoing mission to heal the brokenhearted, to proclaim freedom for captives, and to set free those who are oppressed, bruised, and crushed by tragedy.[6]

This is my favorite thing about living and loving by faith: The evidence of God's love shows up everywhere. If you cultivate the tiny but mighty habit of looking for God in every situation, you'll discover that He is constantly at work for good in this great universe.

It's important to understand that God didn't hire a messenger or send some angel to lead His children home. *God came Himself to show us the way.* Jesus suffered abuse, ridicule, rejection, torture, and murder to invite you into His joy and let you find completion in Him. And He did it because *you are worth doing the work.*

With His guidance, wisdom, and power, you'll become equipped to accomplish things that once seemed impossible.

And just in case no one has ever said this to you before:

I'm so sorry for what you've been through. It wasn't right, it wasn't fair, and you didn't deserve it. What happened to you matters because you matter. You may never forget what it feels like to have suffered so much, but you can be well. It can be well with your soul.

You've already come this far. You are a survivor like me—that's how I know you can do this. Recovering from complex trauma is like facing a giant, and it requires courage and faith like you've never known.

If you want to make it to the other side of your sorrow, you'll need to *do the work, have self-compassion, be aware of the choices you have, celebrate hope, take courage, slow down, learn your gifts, find and trust your allies, armor up, train hard, make healing choices,* and *press on toward joy.*

TinyHabit #1: The Maui Habit

Emotions create habits. Your emotions prompt you to respond to things with specific behaviors, creating a network of habits that are systematically maintained.

Here's how it works: When you feel an emotion, you immediately respond in alignment with the habit you've chosen. This habit enables you to maintain or create the life you believe you most deserve. This is how every one of us designs our lives—for better or for worse.

The good news is that once you understand how habits work, you can design the ones you want and systematically reverse engineer and eliminate the ones you don't.

Habits can take root immediately—not in twenty-one days, or whatever the number is that's currently being promoted as the time it takes to create a new habit. Any parent who has given their child a tablet or cell phone knows that new habits can be created in an instant.

Behavior and habits happen in sequence. In order to design your new, good TinyHabits, you only need to remember to "recode" things toward the good outcome you want to experience.

It's as easy as **ABC**. (**C** is my favorite! It's how we create "Shine" everyday! More on this in chapter 3.)

First, there's a prompt that serves as an Anchor Moment (**A**). The behavior that immediately follows is the habit. For example, when you feel sincerely happy (emotion), you will probably immediately smile (tiny, habitual response).

It's important that as you design new, good habits toward your recovery, the healthy TinyHabit you choose *immediately* follows the Anchor Moment.

And it must be tiny and simple. Break that behavior down to its simplest form. The tinier the better—even one push-up is better than none. Big moves don't work when it comes to sustained lifestyle changes for good.

Your Anchor Moment must be an existing behavior in your daily life—a part of your everyday routine, such as brushing your teeth, using the bathroom, or starting your car.

One of my favorite Anchor Moments is the act of waking up—it's simple and so easy. To begin your journey into the art of TinyHabits, you'll need to identify your Anchor Moments.

For example, your Anchor Moment could be one of the following:

> turning off the alarm
> picking up your phone
> waking up and putting your feet on the floor
> turning on the shower
> getting dressed
> brushing your teeth
> making your bed
> starting your coffee or tea
> waking up your child
> going down the stairs
> walking into the kitchen
> turning on the light
> moving into a different room in your home
> going to the bathroom
> taking a drink of water
> seeing your child
> hearing your phone chime
> _____
> _____
> _____

Once you've identified your (**A**)nchor Moments, you're ready to create your first TinyHabit recipe by choosing the Tiny (**B**)ehavior and Tiny (**C**)elebration to wire the new habit into your brain.

My first TinyHabit is very special to me. It represents the beginning of a whole new way of life and freedom I'd never known. It's kind of like the way Mr. Krabs in *SpongeBob SquarePants* feels about his first dime.[7]

The TinyHabit is called the Maui Habit.[8] And it's so simple! Always remember, it's as easy as **ABC**. And it goes like this:

> Anchor Moment:

After I wake up and put my feet on the floor . . .

> Tiny Behavior (more on this soon):

I will say out loud, "It's going to be a great day."

> Celebration and Shine (my favorite part!):

To wire the habit into my brain, I will immediately smile. 😄 *(And slowly take a deep breath.)*

When I first began working toward mastering my own TinyHabits, Dr. Fogg taught me to modify the Maui Habit to make it easier. As I worked toward mastery, as Dr. Fogg taught me, I would add the word *somehow* to my Tiny Behavior.

"It's going to be a great day—somehow."

Alternately, you may choose a statement that reminds you of your favorite quote or Scripture.

I share more on the TinyHabit of Celebration and Shine (as well as learning to breathe) in chapter 3. For now, think of it as clicking the "like" button on your own social media post—*it's the same reward system that instantly creates our digital habits.*

If you're waking up and immediately feeling sorrow—the way I did before I mastered TinyHabits—know that there is nothing wrong with your mind. In fact, your mind and emotions are working exactly as they were lovingly designed to. They are alerting you to an area of your soul that needs care and should no longer be ignored, pushed aside, or numbed out.

I recognize that you may be in a place emotionally that makes this whole concept seem ridiculous. But please stay with me here: *To your mind, the Maui Habit is a tiny seed of hope.* And when it comes to moving forward in recovery, tiny is all you need. In many ways, it's exactly what you need and right on time.

Think of how a similar but opposite statement such as "I hate my life" plants a poisonous seed in your soul. It automatically sets a destructive system into action as it recycles and churns up your old pain and then sends its stink gushing and sloshing into your brand-new day.

"It's going to be a great day" is a seed that deserves a Tiny Celebration! It celebrates you! The day is great because you're still here, and God is with you—whether you feel it or not.

One of my newest TinyHabits (of hundreds) is waking up and saying a tiny prayer: *Good morning, Father.* This reminds my heart first thing that God is with me and I'm never alone. I celebrate by smiling and taking a deep inhale and a slow exhale as if through an imaginary straw. This is a proven way to calm your nervous system if you struggle with PTSD (post-traumatic stress disorder), as I do. (More on this later.)

By reading this chapter, you've completed an amazing step in your healing journey, and as soon as you begin practicing your first TinyHabit, you will have successfully taken another. Great work today—well done!

Let's keep moving forward for good!

Chapter 2

STRINGS AND MACROS

The Secret Power of Self-Compassion

*There's a big difference between self-compassion and self-pity.
One can empower you to move forward with a fresh perspective,
and the other always and only holds you back.*

MIRACLES HAPPEN EVERY DAY. You woke up this morning. Your heart is beating and your lungs are inhaling and exhaling—and you didn't have to do a thing. You didn't even have to think about it. That's a miracle—just like the day you were born.

Because you woke up this morning, you've been gifted with a miraculous opportunity: the chance to recommit to and take another tiny step in your healing journey.

I imagine that if you're struggling in sorrow, this statement might cause you to feel a bit of frustration. And that's okay—that's the right way to feel about the injustice that created this situation you never would have chosen.

I do hope you'll push past this frustration and consider the truth within the thought that every waking moment of the new day offers hundreds of opportunities to break down some bad coping habits and move toward good, healthy aspirations. The key to break-through is all about what you decide to focus on in this moment.

One of my favorite illustrations of this concept comes from a scene in one of the many *Avengers* sequels: *Age of Ultron*. In this scene, Bruce Banner, who continually struggled with becoming or not becoming the Incredible Hulk, is having a conversation with Black Widow.

As he awkwardly tries to avoid connecting with her about the deeper issues in his heart, she calmly responds, "All my friends are fighters, and here comes this guy [who] spends his life avoiding the fight because he knows he'll win."[1]

Every one of us struggles with this kind of fatalistic think-ing on some level from time to time. But when you're trapped in sadness and sorrow, your mind races onto the road of negativity, discouragement, despair, and defeat before you even set your feet on the floor. That's why sometimes just getting out of bed feels like too much to handle.

It happens so fast and unconsciously that often you have no time to consider the fact that you are an amazing and powerful person gifted with a mind capable of astounding things. If you're completely honest with yourself, you know that every tiny, victorious step toward healing will mean new responsibilities and a new identity.

Change leads to change, and for most people, change is a scary thing. This is a truth of the human condition that creates an under-current of fear in all our lives. Most people have deeply rooted fears of the unknown. You've probably heard a bit about how these fears play out—the whole fight-flight-or-freeze phenomenon.[2]

But even though change can be scary, it's important to understand that fear of the unknown is healthy. I'm going to show you how to use that fear as a reminder to slow down and face reality.

Your life will immediately begin to change as you incrementally recover from your trauma. You can decide right now that you won't allow fear of the unknown to keep you from moving forward.

Party on the Stairs

Alice was a woman who struggled every day with major depressive disorder caused by childhood sexual abuse perpetrated by a neighbor and so-called family friend. When she told her parents, they didn't believe her. She never fully healed from this all-too-common double-abuse scenario.

Decades later, when she was in her fifties, she was placed in yet another inpatient psychiatric program. (This was by no means the first time she'd become a danger to herself and her loved ones.) At first, she resisted treatment in every way, but in time, she began to improve. With a caring staff, controlled diet, medication, and support group meetings, she seemed energetic and hopeful for the first time in her life.

When loved ones visited, she shared things they'd never known. She told them that she wanted to take steps toward finishing her nursing degree so she could help others. Everyone was encouraged and rejoiced at her progress. In time, she was allowed to return home. But within two weeks, she began to regress—hard.

With fresh determination, Alice systematically and intentionally resumed her destructive habits, thoughts, and behaviors. The idea of being well and the responsibilities that came with it were too much for her, and she gave in.

She knew exactly what behaviors to resume in order to reacquire her previous lifestyle of sorrow. And so she turned back to the familiar: what she knew she could accomplish and the heartbreaking life she believed she most deserved.

Maybe she didn't understand that this is a common pattern for trauma survivors, so she had no knowledge about or self-compassion for her struggle and fall.

Like in Alice's experience, the elevated good feelings created by our hopes, dreams, and aspirations are like a staircase. With each step that you climb upward toward your good objective, you feel empowered and motivated to keep going.

For example, imagine it's New Year's Day and you're ready for a change! You see the objective and you're pumped! This is when you may even cheerfully skip a few steps on that imaginary staircase as the motivation wave sweeps you forward!

But when discouragement caused by fears of the unknown shows up—as it always does—it can be the emotional equivalent of falling backward down that flight of stairs. And if there is an abuser who remains in your life, you might even be pushed back down your aspirational staircase.

This is one of the reasons tiny steps are so effective for achieving and sustaining long-term growth in recovery. Because the progress is tiny, when the time comes, you don't have as far to stumble. And these are wide steps—there's a celebration on each one. As you work toward mastery and your new lifestyle, you can enjoy parties on the TinyHabit staircase that are so much fun you'll be excited to wake up each day and enjoy them!

Even if you occasionally stumble or stagger back for any reason, you know that you have a system for recovery that works. And you know that you're going to be okay, because TinyHabits are simple and fun, and your mind is designed to go back to things that work and feel good. As you practice, you'll discover that it's easier to get back on track and keep moving forward.

Self-Pity, Self-Sabotage, and Learned Helplessness

As you begin to win the day—one tiny choice at a time—you'll soon come to a very important crossroads. It's the same crossroads the Incredible Hulk was facing in his conversation with Black Widow.

It's the place where you have to decide whether or not you're willing to surrender something secret and deeply hidden yet very precious to you: the *victim identity*.

The victim identity is a carefully cultivated protective persona. Over time it becomes comfortable because it feels safe and normal. This identity causes a person to become so self-focused and defensive that they incrementally push everyone away—even people they want to love, connect with, and grow closer to.

The victim identity makes the person seek attention and often leads them to commiserate with others about the pain. Or the identity will cause them to choose isolation, believing the lie that a hidden heart is a protected heart.

Many trauma survivors unconsciously create, nurture, and feed this secret identity because it feels like a very strange kind of justice for the abuses they've suffered.

It entices you to live your life drunk, numb, and controlled by your self-pity, and it invites ample opportunity to gain the sympathy of others. This sympathy (and the attention that comes with it) are addictive and affirming in all the wrong ways for everyone involved.

The victim identity is so much easier to accept and understand than are the often uncomfortable, unfamiliar feelings that come with every tiny step you take toward wellness. This sneaky persona is often the reason many people choose to live out their days caring for, hanging out with, and feeding the three most destructive houseguests ever: self-pity, self-sabotage, and learned helplessness.

Self-pity keeps you focused on what's wrong and what you don't have. Self-sabotage reminds you how to go back to the unhealthy life you deeply believe you most deserve. Learned helplessness justifies and excuses your decision to give up by telling you that you have no options and no hope for recovery.

When these three states of mind show up together, the years tick by as the four of you bundle up under the victim identity and stream movies about who is to blame.

The Secret Power of Self-Compassion

One of the most difficult assignments I was given by my trauma therapist was to go out and purchase a little brown baby doll with a head full of beautiful, black, curly hair. My homework was to take good care of her for as long as I needed to in order to take the next step in my healing journey.

Caring for my little robot Baby Alive doll every day was one of the hardest things I've ever done in recovery, but it was also one of the most helpful healing assignments I've been given.

I'll never forget the first time I unboxed her. After carefully releasing her from the little plastic restraints that secured her in the cardboard box, I picked up the little plastic comb and styled her hair a bit before I pushed the button in the middle of her chest. She immediately began talking:

"I don't feel well," she said. "Am I okay?"

I burst into sobbing tears, held her close, and replied, "No, you're not okay. But we will be. Because I'm going to take good care of you."

Being there for her each day when she cried helped me have compassion for the abused six-month-old baby deep inside me who I hadn't realized was still crying.

That little baby girl inside me was hurt and afraid because she believed no one was ever coming to help. I was a severely neglected and abused infant and child, and holding and caring for the baby—including bandaging up her left hand and arm (the places where I have second-degree-burn scars)—helped me deeply understand the importance of self-compassion in the healing journey.

As I cared for my baby doll each day, I realized that healing was happening deep within me. A six-month-old can never understand the pain of being burned and the fear of a world where even babies aren't always safe. Only an adult has the capacity to try to understand how to cope with and recover from something like this. Going this deep, even as an adult (as my trauma therapist often reminds me), takes courage and a lot of faith in the process.

One of my favorite Scriptures says, "Speak out on behalf of the voiceless, and for the rights of all who are vulnerable."[3] And who is more vulnerable than a baby? This very difficult exercise I was given helped me move toward my healing and cultivated in me a deep appreciation for the valuable habit of self-compassion.

As I practiced my strategic TinyHabit of journaling, I learned how to honor the feelings I'd never taken time to process. In time, I created a constellation of TinyHabits (building from the Maui Habit) that incrementally calmed my soul in ways I'd never expected.

Even if I just wrote out one sentence prompted by the memory of the pain, it encouraged me to keep moving forward. I also checked in weekly with my trauma therapist for guidance and prompts for journaling.

I'm happy to report that a very proactive year later, the crying inside stopped. My faith grew, and the river of joy inside me became deeper and stronger than ever.

This is one of the primary reasons that self-compassion is much different from self-pity. Compassion means having genuine concern for the sufferings of others and coming alongside them in order to help bear the burdens they're facing.

Having self-compassion means being willing to intentionally and strategically come alongside yourself in ways that help you better understand your stress responses. It's about acknowledging that every part of your story matters.

Without professional guidance and self-compassion, there may still be a part of you that's crying inside and needs help and loving care. But you'll never know unless you're willing to slow down, go to the very hard places in your story, and embrace the parts of you that are crying out for attention, healing, hope, and love.

Self-compassion is an art, and you've got to be very careful with it. This kind of recovery work is best guided by a professional, because without loving accountability, it could push you dangerously close to self-pity. Without help from people you trust, that road reinforces your victim identity and takes you in circles. (Ever wonder why you have the same thoughts and conversations over and over again about your trauma with very little evidence of progress in recovery?)

At the end of this chapter, I'll provide you with some suggestions for how to create TinyHabits toward self-compassion, but for the serious heart work you'll need professional guidance. Specifically, you will need a PTSD-trained trauma-recovery specialist.[4]

As you take each step forward, you'll soon realize how the secret power of self-compassion empowers you with a fresh perspective that can lead to growth, healing, and freedom—while self-pity always and only holds you back.

Do You Want to Be Made Well?

There is a passage of Scripture that tells us of the time when Jesus was walking through the streets of Jerusalem near the Sheep Gate and arrived at the pool of Bethesda. This was a place where crowds of sick, blind, lame, or paralyzed people lay on the porches waiting for miracles of healing.

The local legend said that an angel of the Lord would visit the pool from time to time and stir up the water. The first person to step in as soon as the water began to bubble up would be healed of any and every disorder.

One man had been lying next to this pool, sick, for thirty-eight years.

> When Jesus saw him and knew he had been ill for a long time, he asked him, "Would you like to get well?"
>
> "I can't, sir," the sick man said, "for I have no one to put me into the pool when the water bubbles up. Someone else always gets there ahead of me."
>
> Jesus told him, "Stand up, pick up your mat, and walk!"
>
> Instantly, the man was healed! He rolled up his sleeping mat and began walking![5]

This Scripture offers a perfect example of what someone who is stuck in self-pity would say when faced with the very real opportunity to be well.

Did you notice his victim-identity mindset and the language of self-pity? He said to Jesus, "I have no one." But clearly this wasn't true. He couldn't walk, so how did he get there in the first place?

At some time in the past—maybe even on that very day, unless he stayed there at the pool 24/7 (which, I suppose, after that many years could have been true)—someone had helped him.

This first excuse is a good example of how, when we're blinded by our pain, we're often unable to see, appreciate, or receive the loving care of those who are sincerely trying to help. Remember, the victim identity pushes others away in order to protect itself from the possibility of more pain.

Maybe you know what I'm describing here. Notice how he completely discounted the fact that Jesus was right there, noticing him, caring about him, spending time with him, and talking with him.

He completely overlooked the fact that this was finally his chance! The person who was right there with him was offering him the next step in his healing journey.

It seems to me that he believed his problem was everybody else's fault. He said, "Someone else always gets there ahead of me." People who live with a victim identity always find a reason to blame someone else—this relieves the burden of focusing on what they can do for themselves. Still, Jesus saw this man's heart, just as He sees and knows yours.

Jesus knew that the man was finally ready to accept the responsibilities that would come with this step toward healing. I believe that's why He singled him out, and why this one man's healing story has been preserved and shared for thousands of years for you and me to benefit from today.

Did you notice the three tiny suggestions Jesus offered? "Stand up, pick up your mat, and walk!" Even if the man had taken *one* of these tiny actions, he would have accomplished something miraculous! It started with his tiny—yet transformative—decision to believe.

You're Not Trash

When it comes to creating TinyHabits that will allow you to navigate toward wholeness in recovery, you will have to choose to recognize and be mindful of when you are responding with self-pity.

That decision will help you regroup and refocus on self-compassion, which can empower you to face the fear of responsibility that comes with being well.

The longer you've been trapped in sorrow, the more your identity becomes defined by sadness. To leave it behind creates a great deal of uncertainty as you wonder, *Who am I without my sadness?* The decision to stay in the darkness and fear feels like a safer choice. That's why so often when we have the information about the next right thing we need to do, we still don't do it.

This is probably why so many are caught in the diet-and-exercise hamster wheel. We know what needs to be done, and we have more information, websites, apps, and plans than we can count—but still we struggle.

In Behavior Design, we call this the *information-action fallacy*. It's proof that having information, depending on willpower, and setting goals are not enough. What we need are carefully designed personal strategies that lead to the *identity shift*.

Going in circles on the road of self-pity; repeating the same mistakes; having the same arguments; telling the same stories; and reliving, repackaging, and recreating the drama are easy. Do them enough, and they become automatic bad habits. Staying in these habits is easier and a lot more comfortable than moving toward an identity shift because they are what you already know.

If you'd like a fun, visual way to see this concept in action, I suggest watching the first forty-five minutes of Pixar's *Toy Story 4*.

It's the story of a character who was literally made from the trash gathered from a little plastic garbage can in the corner of a kindergarten classroom. Moments after his maker, little Bonnie, finishes crafting him into a toy, names him Forky, and writes her name onto the bottom of his little wooden popsicle feet, he springs to life!

But pay careful attention to the way Forky begins a resolute quest to return to the trash. Day and night he works toward his objective. He doesn't understand that now he's truly alive and has a home and a community of toys (his new family) who want to love and spend time with him.

Forky fights hard, even skipping out on sleep to try to get back into the trash. When Woody, the toy who is trying to look after Forky, asks why, he responds, "It's warm. It's cozy. And safe!"

Forky doesn't understand that it's trash and he does not have to live there anymore.[6]

That Pixar team gets me every time! Really great storytelling there. Think about how many of us can relate to Forky.

One of the best things about applying TinyHabits to faith is that they are safe. Regardless of your ability level, you can carry out each new TinyHabit successfully every time! Even though there will be some trial and error, you can never fail. Just the creation of the TinyHabit will be celebrated for what it is: a tiny victory toward wellness.

I can say that with confidence for two reasons: (1) You are going to be the one to design the perfect TinyHabits for you, and (2) God doesn't make trash. You were born to win.

Strings, Loops, and Macros: How the Brain Processes Information

I've been fascinated with the human mind for as long as I can remember. When my son was diagnosed with autism shortly before his third birthday, all my extensive, ongoing studies on cognition came in very handy.

From the moment we left the children's hospital, I began working continually to design strategies to help him accomplish even the smallest tasks.

At first, he had to learn how to speak in simple, two-word sentences. I knew this was something he really wanted to do, and I saw his frustration when he couldn't. He was trying his very best, *yet he lacked the skills*.

I understood that for him to acquire the skills, we'd need to start very, very small—we needed to take baby steps.

My research toward this tiny practice for my son and in my own trauma-recovery work led to breakthroughs for both of us and would eventually be verified through the science of Behavior Design. I know this process works.

As I mentioned before, every computer program is made up of thousands or even millions of tiny symbols grouped together into strings, loops, and macros. In programming, a *string* is a group or sequence of characters, like a sentence. A *loop* is a sequence of instructions that repeats until a certain condition is achieved, and *macros* are automatic-input sequences that help with efficiency and speed. Our minds are very similar in the way that we process information. At an estimated four hundred billion bits of information per second, your mind processes information in loops, paths, and sequences.

In other words, if you're stuck in sadness, you've got thousands of bad cognitive habits repeating like a bad program over and over again, all day, every day. This why I say that *trauma is bad code*.

In time, you incrementally develop the victim identity and mentality. And in order to maintain it, you will always need an oppressor, so you wake up and begin to oppress and suppress *yourself* because you think it's the life you deserve.

The good news is that your thoughts are not who you are. You can provide fresh input and fresh data, and new, helpful thoughts and behaviors will increasingly follow.

And you don't have to make huge changes to participate in your recovery, because for breakthrough, it's the accumulated, incremental, tiny changes that lead to lasting change and sustained joy.

My son is now an honor-roll student. He also speaks conversational Japanese and is in his fourth year of working toward his pilot's license—but he started out as a hardworking toddler.

Striving through years of frustrated, often tear-filled struggles, we didn't give up. We worked together consistently every day. I took everything we were learning from his professional team and created customized TinyHabit strategies that we built into his daily home life and culture. This is how he first learned how to accomplish two-word sentences and formed new pathways in his brain each day. He still has struggles because of autism, but now he is in the habit of creating and celebrating strategies that work for him, based on his abilities.

In the same way, your healing journey will require a unique strategy, intentionally created TinyHabits, repetition, and celebration so you can form new habits and new ways of thinking. You don't have to be another PTSD or childhood-trauma statistic. You can beat the odds.

Your Identity Shift

Accepting that your mind is designed to learn and grow through baby steps—one of the reasons we begin life as babies—can help you begin designing your own new paths.

In time, your new habits will lead to what we call the *identity shift*. Without this shift, you will stay stuck. But there is always hope. As my son did, you have to commit to your healing journey and start at the very beginning. So let's do this.

Your identity (begin the *Mission: Impossible* theme song here), if you choose to accept it, is simply this: You are loved.

Yes: short, simple, tiny. There it is—your brand-new identity! What do you think? I'll tell you right now: It looks great on you!

Your willingness to receive this will empower you to take your next tiny step. The peace of mind and joy you crave are identity features that flow from your essential belief about who you are and what you believe you're worth.

An identity shift from *victim* to *beloved* is the key to freedom because you will design the life you believe you deserve.

If, at a subconscious level, you believe you are worthless and unloved, you will work every day to prove yourself right. This is a common psychological habit. We all love to be right, and when we think we are, our first instinct is to look for evidence to prove it. It works for both positive and negative thinking.

If you're finally finished with the way that the mindset of feeling worthless has impacted your life, you're ready for your next level.

You were created by someone who loves you: God created you to love you and to enable you to overflow His love to others. You are a part of His good work in this world, but you must decide to be willing to step into and live out of your true core identity: You are loved.

Please think for a minute about what you believe to be your identity. What is it that you believe is most true about yourself?

Within the autism community, we are very familiar with what's called PDD (pervasive developmental disorder). This is a neurological disorder that affects every part of a child's social, communicative, nutritive, and everyday practical-living skills.

Similarly, sadness and sorrow can also be pervasive—so much so that you may be struggling to remember who you are as a person apart from the situations and circumstances that have left you so brokenhearted.

Would you agree that your sadness and sorrow are affecting every part of your life in some way? If so, that's pervasive.

I wrote this chapter to offer you the opportunity to consider and choose a very simple, tiny strategy toward recovery—I invite you to consider accepting your new identity: You are loved.

I pray that you'll stop hiding from this fight. With the right tools and strategies, *you will win.*

TinyHabit #2: The Perfect Tiny Behaviors

Congratulations on making it to the end of chapter 2! I won't bore you with the data on how few people make it this far, but I will tell you that you are now an honored member of the I-bought-a-new-book-and-actually-read-it society! It's a real thing—I think there's even a Facebook group for it!

Now, this chapter is filled with some pretty heavy stuff, right? I hope the self-pity, self-sabotage, learned-helplessness crew has been evicted. It's time to spend that energy focusing on the truth about your new identity.

Remember, designing TinyHabit recipes is as easy as **ABC**.

You've already identified many of your morning Anchor Moments. Now schedule time to grow that list to identify Anchor Moments for the afternoon, early evening, and late evening as well.

Now it's time to add the best Tiny Behavior to the recipe. Because we are focusing on your brand-new, super simple identity alignment, I'll use the example of saying out loud, "I am loved" immediately following the Anchor Moment. Remember to choose an Anchor Moment that's a part of your existing routine.

There's something about speaking out loud that's supernatural.[7] Once you've spoken something, it can never be taken back. It is released into the world—it's real.

For your newest TinyHabit toward faith, try it out. Just speak it aloud: "I am loved."

In order for this courageous affirmation to take root, carry out this Tiny Behavior immediately after the Anchor Moment. Always remember the sequence: **A, B, C.**

Then you must immediately include the Tiny Celebration, which wires the habit into your brain. The table on page 40 offers a few sample recipes to get you started.

If you want to use the same TinyHabit you used in chapter 1, feel free!

I think of this as stacking the TinyHabits for maximum effectiveness. It's fun—like leveling up in a video game.

I say, "It's going to be a great day—because I am loved!" I follow this with a smile, and I turn my palms up and say, "Thank You, God."

It's important to continue to affirm your new identity at every opportunity. It's a simple TinyHabit to stack because it takes no time to say it or think about it.

Simplicity changes behavior, so keep it simple. You don't need a personal mission statement here—just a quick, simple, short phrase.

Another great level-up secret is that if you anchor your new

Anchor Moment	Tiny Behavior	Celebration (Shine! 😁)
After I brush my teeth,	I will say, "I am loved"	and smile at myself in the mirror.
After I take a sip of coffee or tea,	I will say, "I am loved"	and smile and take a deep breath.
After I start my car,	I will say, "I am loved"	and smile and place my hand on my heart.
After I stop at a traffic light,	I will say, "I am loved"	and smile and say, "I'm awesome."
After I pick up my phone,	I will say, "I am loved"	and smile and say, "God is good."
After I put on my shoes,	I will say, "I am loved"	and smile and say, "Thank You, God."

Tiny Behavior to a tiny event that happens multiple times a day—such as getting in and out of the car, going to the bathroom, or taking a sip of your coffee—*the habit will wire in even faster.*

I know it seems so tiny, so small, this new habit you're designing. But each time you choose this, your mind will begin creating new pathways—one tiny choice at a time. It's similar to debugging an erroneous line of code and replacing it with a new one.

Remember, our emotions create our habits, one Tiny Behavior anchored to another. Then they are reinforced by affirmations in the same way that babies who are born into healthy, loving homes learn to walk, speak, eat, and understand their worth and value in this world.

If you're like me and you weren't dealt the safe, healthy home card, please don't let that stop you from drawing new cards, one after the next, as you discard the old ones—for good.

I can't express enough the importance of affirmation and celebration. We change for good through positive reinforcement, not negative. So always include a Tiny Celebration in your TinyHabit recipe. It won't work without it.

It's sad but true: Far too many of us were unnurtured, unparented, abused, and neglected as children. That will never be fair or okay. But we're *not* victims for life, and it's perfectly okay to love, nurture, and care for yourself as an adult. With practice and commitment, your new TinyHabits for good become pervasive and beneficial in all the right ways.

One of my favorite personal examples is how I used TinyHabits to create a Master Plan for grief and trauma recovery, and I subsequently lost fifteen pounds in about six weeks. My loving self-care TinyHabits replaced the sugar addiction I'd picked up after my mother died. I haven't seen that sugar habit since! Goodbye, and good riddance!

Awesome job today daring to believe and speak the truth that you are loved. Wow! That's two TinyHabits to celebrate right there! Keep up the great work!

Chapter 3

THE CURSE THAT'S A GIFT

The Superpower of Free Will

*Isn't it amazing that the answer to what it means to be human
lies in the smallest, youngest creatures—our babies?*

BABIES, A NETFLIX ORIGINAL DOCUMENTARY SERIES

As A BABY, you drank in the fullness of life unlike at any other time. The continual procession of first experiences—the tastes, sounds, feelings, scents, and sights—flooded over you and surrounded you with multisensory information.

Though you had no language or ability to describe or understand what was happening, you had to quickly learn how to process and make sense of it all in order to survive.

In many ways, we all know a bit about what it would be like to arrive on a strange and mysterious planet. We've all experienced instant immersion into a brand-new civilization called planet Earth. It happened the moment you were born!

It's truly amazing how much information babies can process—and it's no wonder humans need so much sleep in our early years of life. *It's all so exhausting!*

During those formative years, we begin building our lives and identities based on what information we choose to keep or discard. It's a habit that never leaves us.

Every second of every day, this subconscious habit continues: choosing what we will retain or discard. Will you say yes or no? These two basic choices fuel every decision and behavior, and what you choose creates the emotions and habits that accumulate into your present reality.

In many ways, it's a lot like the binary number system used by computers: zeros and ones. It's on or off, keep or discard, focus or ignore, yes or no.

In 1999, *The Matrix* was a big deal to me and just about every other sci-fi fan on the planet. The mass appeal was amplified by the fact that you couldn't watch it without spending some time afterward wondering what reality actually is.

In one of the most iconic scenes, Morpheus, the leader of the rebellion, is hoping to recruit Neo, the man they believe to be the chosen one. Morpheus explains to Neo that there's an alternate, actual reality available to him. And he makes an offer:

> You take the blue pill, the story ends. You wake up in your bed and believe whatever you want to believe. You take the red pill, you stay in Wonderland, and I show you how deep the rabbit hole goes.[1]

Along the way on my healing journey, I've discovered that trauma recovery is very similar to this imagined scenario. When it comes to making progress in the healing journey, even the most strong-willed among us can find ourselves confused, delayed, and occasionally debilitated by a distorted alternate reality that layers of tragedy, trauma, poverty, and abuse can create.

The longer the unhealed places within us are left unaddressed and unprocessed, the more they behave like a swirling vortex or a vacuum pulling everything else toward it. The emotional distortion this creates can warp everything you experience as it clouds and clutters your mind. This happens because pain needs to be acknowledged, attended to, and processed in healthy ways.

Sorrow produced by trauma is not easily ignored, and you can't outrun it by staying busy. You can't fight it by pushing away everyone who cares about you. So what can you do? *You can make a choice.*

Morpheus explains to Neo that one option is to "wake up in your bed and believe whatever you want to believe." And he's right. If you decide to keep on nursing and feeding your sorrow, your story ends—every single tiny time you make that choice.

But you always have a powerful alternative decision you can make: On a moment-by-moment basis, you can choose to fight for your life, one tiny choice at a time.

Be Mindful of Your Thoughts

Have you ever taken the time to consider the reasons why you do what you do and think what you think? Why did you make the last choice you made? The habit of becoming mindful and fully present concerning your decision-making process is powerful.

Free will is a curious gift of love from God. Except for under special conditions, you and I have the ability to choose how we will react or respond based on our beliefs, opinions, and preferences.

Chapter 2 of this book offered you the chance to know the truth about who you are. Remember your identity: *You are loved.*

This is one of the most powerful anchoring beliefs you can have because it's a strong foundation to stand on as you examine the opinions and preferences that determine the next choice you'll make—including the choice to keep reading this chapter.

It's your belief about your identity that determines what you say, who you spend your time with, how you respond to your sorrow, and how you treat yourself and others.

Every second of your waking hours, since you were a baby, you have been expressing who you are by what you choose. And this is a very good thing! In fact, it's a great thing, because the more you understand the power of the choices you make, the more empowered you'll feel to create habits that will shift you into a healing mindset—a lifestyle of choosing faith, hope, gratitude, service, and love.

These are the identity features that power a life of transcendent, overcoming faith along with sustained peace, soul rest, and contagious joy.

It's always worth the time to use the gift of free will to contribute to what's good in any given situation—to be part of the solution to a conflict instead of part of the problem. As Obi-Wan Kenobi cautioned a young Anakin Skywalker, you must remain ever "mindful of your thoughts."[2]

If you forget that you always have a choice about how you respond, you're more likely to lean toward unhealthy responses to stress, trauma, and grief, which is why I believe that free will can be both a blessing and a curse. As I mentioned earlier, it's a curious gift.

So Many Choices

I have a friend who is from Nagaland, a state between China, India, and Myanmar. Having been severely politically, emotionally, and economically oppressed for generations, they are a people without a sense of belonging, and they have historically dealt with a great deal of injustice, abuse, and trauma.

When I met my friend, he was selling DIRECTV. As a new mom stuck at home all the time, I was *so* excited when he called to talk with me that day! I didn't buy the satellite service, but we've kept in touch ever since.

Back then, he was working long hours to support both his immediate and extended family. I'll never forget his response when I asked him for his opinion of American culture based on what he knew of life in the United States.

After a long pause, he replied, "You all have so many choices."

I hadn't thought about it until he said this, but it's true. Just stop by the bread aisle in the local superstore and take note of the many options for something as basic as bread. I actively avoid superstores for this reason. It stresses me out sometimes. How can there be a hundred different kinds of bread?

Decision fatigue is real. But we're used to it here because it's a part of our normal. It's always a blessing to have options, but it becomes a curse when, for whatever reason, we decide not to choose wisely.

By this I mean that it's a curse when we choose to live our lives on autopilot—unconscious, unwilling to put in the work, and blissfully unaware of our purpose and what we're truly capable of.

In the video-gaming community, we identify characters who repeat the same lines no matter how many times you talk to them as *non-player characters* or *NPCs*. They're not helpful, and they just take up space—they're basically part of the scenery. After the first few conversations, they repeat themselves and waste your time. Maybe this reminds you of someone you know.

We always have the freedom to choose how we will respond to any situation, person, or feeling. Instead, we trick ourselves into thinking we are powerless and have no options. If we believe this lie, we start to be rewired into NPCs, our stories become severely limited, and our contributions to the greater story God is writing in and through us drops to nearly nothing.

But if we remove the reality-distortion filter created by our sorrow, we'll be able to see that we always have a choice or two—or a few!

The decision to stay stuck is a choice, but every time you make a healing choice toward good—no matter how tiny—you win that moment. With practice and determination, by the time you lie down at night, you've won the day.

Your TinyHabits will accumulate into a lifestyle of victory. And your Tiny Celebrations will produce an increase of peace, hope, and joy—one tiny choice at a time.

A Temptation Inventory

One of the first things Jesus did when He started to teach and preach to the crowds was to clearly explain who He is and what He came to accomplish. He's direct like that. One day, not long after He began to make public appearances, Jesus went straight to the front of the synagogue and clearly announced that He was on a mission "to proclaim good news to the poor . . . to proclaim freedom for the prisoners and recovery of sight for the blind, to set the oppressed free."[3] That announcement is still circling the globe. God wants you to choose faith in Him so He can empower and guide you to keep moving forward toward true freedom.

I'm no stranger to the temptations you may be facing because of your sadness and sorrow. I've found it a most helpful endeavor to schedule time to do what I call a *temptation inventory*.

It's easy. You can journal or use a spreadsheet (if that's your thing) to map out and identify the temptations you're dealing with in recovery. As you do this, keep in mind that temptation is never the thing that separates you from God's best. The temptation is not the sin—the temptation is only the prompt (or notification) to remain mindful and alert of the need to respond strategically toward what's good and helpful.

Here are some common temptations that can get in the way of recovery:

> the temptation to believe you're all alone

> the temptation to believe that no good can come from what you've lost or what you've been through
> the temptation to believe that your experiences have no meaning and no redemptive possibilities
> the temptation to believe that no one cares and no one could possibly understand
> the temptation to believe that you can't afford to get help when, really, you can't afford not to
> the temptation to believe that you don't have time for wellness or self-care

All these are lies.

They are the erroneous beliefs that construct the walls and mirrors of the place I call the *psychological fun house mirror maze* in your mind. It's a place of total reality distortion designed and constructed from multiple layers of grief.

But there is meaning in the madness. Your choice to begin to nurture your willing heart today is exactly the step you need in the right direction—a step toward strategies that will help you accept your losses and grieve and process in healthy ways. For example:

> seeking out the right trauma specialist
> finding a Celebrate Recovery or other safe support group[4]
> texting someone you trust to break the silence and share your story

> committing to your new TinyHabits to reprogram your
mind and take control of your reactions and responses

What Are You Looking For?

This process begins with finding out exactly what you've lost. It's
incredibly healing and honoring to slow down and focus on what
you're missing. Please make time to figure out specifically what the
situation has cost you.

Are you grieving the fact that you will never have a certain
relationship you've longed for? Are you missing the justice you crave
for the abuses you've suffered? What is it about a loved one that you
once treasured the most that's no longer a part of your life?

To slow down and make note of these things validates your
feelings and acknowledges the sources of your pain. This gives you
a starting point for your recovery. Only after you understand what
you've lost can you stop looking for something unknown and stop
accepting substitutes for what you really need.

If you're practicing your new TinyHabits, then you're already
taking sure steps to stop numbing your pain in unhealthy ways.
Composing your temptation inventory and understanding how to
use the gift of free will are loving behaviors that will provide insights
into the complexities of your story. They are like points of light—if
you follow them, they will surely lead you out of this present darkness.

Think back to *The Matrix*. Do you see how if you choose to
stay stuck where you are, the story really does end?

When you decide to give up and give in, you know exactly how
every new minute is going to unfold—you know it will be exactly

like the last. You've committed to living out that old, painful script and story. You've made your choice: You've lost. Every time you decide it's not worth the work, you lose more of yourself.

The instant you decide to take the next brave step toward healing, you'll find that the "rabbit hole" really is deep, but the journey is worth it because you're worth it.

You are made in the image of God, and you're beloved by Him. You deserve to find the joy and abundant life of faith that you were created to experience and enjoy.[5]

Long before the Wachowskis wrote the screenplay for *The Matrix*, a man named Moses stood before an enormous, traumatized, and tired crowd of people who'd recently been delivered from generations of slavery, bondage, and oppression. Like Morpheus, Moses offered the people before him a choice: "I've brought you today to the crossroads of Blessing and Curse"[6]—blessing if you listen to, believe, and walk out what God says about you and your journey with Him; curse if you don't pay attention and choose to continue to follow only what you already know and believe.

It is a step of faith to believe that God made you to love you and to be with you forever.

It's a step of faith to believe that you do indeed have the ability to master the art of using the superpower of free will to contribute to God's good work in this great universe.[7]

Your ability to choose and remain willing to do the next right thing to move forward in your healing journey empowers you to design a life of peace and joy. I know you can do this, because it's a skill you've had since you were a baby—a skill that no trauma or tragedy can take from you.

Please don't give up. You're doing great, and you're already on your way.

TinyHabit #3: Celebration and Shine!

Steve Jobs, the cofounder of Apple, once shared that he'd been wearing his famous black turtleneck, blue jeans, and New Balance sneakers for well over ten years straight. Though this might seem to be just another one of his quirky personal habits, it's actually a common TinyHabit for entrepreneurs, professional athletes, and others who understand how systems and strategies can enable them to perform at peak levels. It also helps minimize the cognitive overload created by decision fatigue.

Have you noticed that most of the decisions you make that you're least proud of happen when you're physically or cognitively tired? At the end of a long, stressful day, it's hard to be at your best.

When it comes to intentional, strategic trauma recovery, you are dealing with decision fatigue at a higher level. Your mind and body are constantly suppressing the pain caused by your unhealed, unprocessed sorrow. And it's exhausting! You're experiencing fight-flight-or-freeze adrenaline twenty-four hours a day. Your brain is used to staying on alert—it's as if you're being chased by a bear all day.[8]

TinyHabits toward trauma recovery and faith will help you retrain your mind to understand that you are going to be okay. They empower you with fun tools that work.

And I do mean *fun*! Get ready to begin moving toward a lifestyle of joy!

Welcome to the third TinyHabit: Celebration! This is my all-time favorite part of the system.

Now that you've practiced a bit, this is a good spot to go deeper into the anatomy of TinyHabits.

As a review, the transformative power of TinyHabits is as simple as **ABC**:

> Identify your Anchor Moment—that existing routine behavior, such as starting your car.

> Choose a new Tiny Behavior—a scaled-down, tiny, simple version of the new habit that you want to replace the unwanted, trauma-induced habit with.

And now—drumroll, please—it's time for the . . .

> Tiny Celebration! It's time to create Shine!

Did I mention that this is my favorite part? *Shine* is what we call the feeling you experience as you celebrate the execution of the Tiny Behavior immediately following your Anchor Moment! When you complete the second step in your TinyHabit recipe, you must immediately celebrate. *The celebration literally wires the new habit into your brain*. And it feels good!

It's truly amazing—and the science behind it is sound and proven.

That good feeling is caused by a jolt of the feel-good hormone dopamine. Think of the feeling you get when someone likes your photo on Instagram. It's fun and you feel successful, and you're happy that you shared, right? You may even start planning how to do it again!

My big sister is a PhD neuroscientist who works in a lab all day. For decades, she said she had no time for social media. Then we introduced her to Instagram. Now she posts more than I do! She even created an account for her smart car, Ladybug! She's a fan of that Shine.

Or if you're not using social media, think about that feeling you get when a friend hugs you. Or when your spouse smiles at you. Or when your boss gives you a compliment. Or when a stranger on the train waves at you.

That tiny good feeling is the Shine that keeps us going back for more. Our minds crave positive interactions that feel good—just like when we were babies. Those positive affirmations make us feel successful—and when we feel successful, we go back for more.

The best news of all is that you can create your own Shine anytime to reinforce and wire in the good habits you want. And the beauty of mastering Shine is that it often overflows to others.

This tiny feeling of joy produced by celebration is not a new concept. Jesus taught about this when He told His followers to live in such ways that their light would continually shine and help others recognize that God is good.[9]

Thankfully, because God is a systems guy and human behavior is systematic, we can cultivate and master the habit of Celebration systematically for good and for life.

Here's a simple example that builds on some of the earlier recipes:

A: After I brush my teeth . . .

B: I will say out loud, "It's going to be a great day—somehow!"

C: Then I will immediately smile at my reflection in the mirror and say, "Looking good!"

This is going to feel really awkward at first. Remember that you can change the affirmative statement to best suit you. Maybe "Hey there, gorgeous!" or "Looking sharp!"

This was very difficult for me at first. I was in the habit of only seeing and recognizing the negative things about my reflection in the mirror. At one time, I'd been diagnosed with trauma-induced *facial blindness*, meaning that I didn't know what I looked like. I had an impaired ability to recognize my own face.

Learning the TinyHabit of Celebration and the power of Shine enabled me to finally see God's good, artistic work in the mirror. And I know it can work for you, too! Like me, you may feel a little silly at first, but that's great! Silly moments are Shine moments, so the more the better!

No matter how silly or uncomfortable you feel, please don't give up. You don't have to look in the mirror at all if that's too difficult for you at this stage in the healing journey. Just smile and leave it at that. Well done!

No matter how tiny, always celebrate, because you deserve it. And I believe that God is celebrating with you! He delights to see His children celebrating everything that's good—no matter how tiny. He even commands it in the same loving way that we remind kids to brush their teeth and eat their vegetables.

In one of my all-time favorite Scriptures, we read the following:

> You'll do best by filling your minds and meditating on
> things true, noble, reputable, authentic, compelling,
> gracious—the best, not the worst; the beautiful, not
> the ugly; things to praise, not things to curse. Put into
> practice what you learned from me. . . . Do that, and
> God, who makes everything work together, will work you
> into his most excellent harmonies.[10]

If we follow God's system—which includes a lifestyle of Tiny Celebrations—He promises that our peace, love, and faith will surely grow.

But wait, there's more: As we master the habit of Celebration and Shine, we make this world a better place, one tiny choice at a time.

Well done finishing this chapter—you're on your way to joy! Keep moving forward—you've got this!

Chapter 4

THE JOY SET BEFORE YOU
The Thrill of Hope

You know this feeling already: You feel Shine when you ace an exam.
You feel Shine when you give a great presentation and people clap at the end.
You feel Shine when you smell something delicious that you cooked for the
first time. . . . By skillfully celebrating, you create a feeling of Shine, which
in turn causes your brain to encode the new habit.

B. J. FOGG, PHD, *TINY HABITS*

LIFE DOESN'T DEPEND on circumstances from which it needs to draw value. Life inherently has meaning and value. The meaning of your life—which is to love and be loved—holds all the power you need to take the next step in your healing journey.

Understanding this simple truth is the key to victory. You must make the time to learn how to see and love yourself for who you truly are—just as God does.

What would your day be like if you made every decision out of love instead of fear?

What if you chose kindness at every opportunity, even in conflict, simply because you have the ability to? What would the world be like if each of us took every opportunity to be kind?

Kindness is evidence of the presence of God.[1] That's why when we unexpectedly experience authentic—not manipulative—kindness it feels as though time stops. In those moments we feel like life is good and no matter what happens or has happened, somehow, mysteriously, everything just might be okay.

True kindness is not just a trendy, warm-and-fuzzy idea. It's a superpower gift from God by His Spirit. When someone is kind, it communicates the tiny but powerful message that you're valuable and you matter.

Every time I drop my sons off for one thing or another, I encourage them to remember to "be brave, be wise, be mindful, be faithful, and *be kind to yourself* and others because you are so loved."

I hope that you'll consider curating the TinyHabit of being kind to yourself every day. Putting yourself down and rehearsing the pain of your trauma is easy and often automatic. But it takes creativity and innovation to be kind. The time will pass anyway, so why not try something brand-new?

Because kindness takes creativity, every decision you make to be kind to yourself creates brand-new neurological pathways. This process is called *neurogenesis*, and it involves new growth and development of tissue in your brain and nervous system.

I like to describe this phenomenon as the creation of new lines of cognitive "code." Neurogenesis directly affects communication with the hippocampus, which is responsible for memory, emotion, and acquiring new data. This is exactly what you need in order to break free of the pain of your trauma.

When you are creative in your thoughts, it leads to new behaviors that open up new possibilities. This is how you grow in strength, wisdom, peace, and joy—little by little each day.

Innovative, Intentional, and Effective

Take a deep, calming breath in through your nose and slowly out through your mouth, as if you're exhaling through a smoothie straw. You must remember to breathe, because this can be a scary exercise. The slow breathing will calm your nervous system and help you focus.

Now, imagine for a moment what your life will be like as you gain more and more freedom from sadness. Will you . . .

> take up a new hobby?
> move toward your fitness and nutrition goals?
> lead a Bible study at your church?
> start playing the guitar again?
> plant a garden?
> finish your degree?
> begin writing that novel?
> learn a new language?
> start dancing again?
> restore that old car?
> dress up and go to sci-fi conventions?
> go to open mic night?

Whatever it is, start imagining the good future you'd like to design—one TinyHabit after the next.

I've been collecting quotes since high school, and one of my favorites is simply this: "Healthy things grow." Aristotle is sometimes quoted as having said, "Growth is evidence of life." This means that the opposite is also true: *Dead things don't grow—they stay the same or deteriorate.*

If you're stuck in a pattern of being unkind to yourself, tormented by the same negative thoughts and responses because of childhood trauma, then in some key areas of your life you're simply not growing.

Still, there's always good news! Because you woke up this morning, the very next moment of your life—even if it's just the next few seconds—can be an innovative, intentional, and effective tiny step toward healthy growth.

In Behavior Design training, we teach that if you plant the right seed in good soil, it will grow without coaxing. This reminds me of what Jesus taught His disciples about the importance of caring for the "soil" of our souls.[2]

Your new TinyHabits are like seeds, and your mind and emotions are the soil. Having the right seeds, or habits, is never enough. You must also choose every day to take good, loving, intentional care of the soil of your mind and spirit.

Healthy relationships are growing relationships. Just as you would dig a tiny hole in the soil to position a seed and then water it, place it in sunlight, and check on it regularly, you need the same kind of diligent, loving care for growth and healing in your relationship with yourself. Every time you make kind and loving choices to keep moving forward in recovery, you're one step closer to experiencing the healing and rest from sorrow that God wants for your heart, soul, spirit, and mind.

Always think of your new TinyHabits as seeds. The ones that have already taken root and are sprouting are habits you must continue to practice until they become permanent and good parts of your life—in other words, your lifestyle. These become the newest part of your identity of sustainable wellness. They usually produce results that everyone who truly loves you will notice right away. These people will be the ones who say, "Something's different" and "I'm happy for you!"

It's very important to understand that your sadness and sorrow don't mean that you are irreparably damaged. They only mean that you have some untilled soil in the garden of your soul that needs attention. The Bible calls these areas "unplowed ground" in your heart.[3] Sadness and sorrow are symptoms of a sickness of the heart. Right now, you're not well at a heart level, and this means you're in need of special care and conditions in order to heal and grow stronger.

How to Overcome the World

This world in its current state is broken. It's full of trouble and heartache. Yet you now have access to a system that works and can empower you to transcend and overcome any and every kind of sorrow.

The proof of this is found throughout our collective history. Humans are a species with the miraculous ability to survive even the worst traumatic experiences. This may seem impossible and idealistic, but it's true. A supernatural solution in trauma recovery is available, and many hundreds of thousands—even millions—of people have discovered it. These trauma survivors have been empowered and blessed with the ability to persevere and rise above their circumstances and sorrow—no matter how disturbing, evil, and traumatic.

When I visited Dachau as a twelve-year-old, I was too young

to understand what I was feeling. It was oppressive and frightening because it was more than just sadness. It was palpable evil still living there, haunting the emptied gas chambers, ovens, and bunks.

Thankfully, my group and I also spent time in the on-site memorial museum. As I looked at the pictures of thousands of oppressed and abused people, my heart broke. But I also read about many of the survivors. Through their stories, a seed was planted in my heart. I knew that I wanted to learn more about them and what had happened to them after they were liberated from that hell-on-earth experience.

I began to seek out stories of survivors of Hiroshima, Nagasaki, and the Cambodian Killing Fields. I was blessed to work alongside and gain a lifelong friendship with a real-life Wonder Woman, Naren, who survived the horrors of the Khmer Rouge.

Naren told me about how for five years she endured hell before making her courageous escape, walking barefoot for days across minefields. She made up her mind that she wouldn't give up. Starving, bewildered, and clinging to the very edges of life and sanity, she made it to the Cambodian border. There she met a Christian couple who took her in and helped her heal and recover.

At first, she had no idea how she survived. She began to learn English by reading the Bible. As she read the book of Genesis over and over, she began to see that only God is good. He created the world, and He created her. The more she read, the more she realized that Jesus is the Son of God and that He had a plan for her life. She used to call herself a Buddhist, but through the Bible, she met the one true God, who, as she says, "made us to come to

Him. He is the One who hears, sees our hearts, protects, provides, and answers every prayer." As she describes it, Buddha "wears a big smile but is just cement."

Naren hopes that as she shares the tiny parts of her story, others will discover the truth. "It's easy to complain," she says, "but I remind myself: God saved me and led me through. He is the way, the truth, and the life!"[4]

Through my research, studies, and conversations, I learned that Naren and other survivors who recover and find their path to joy have the exact same choices in common:

> They choose to abandon self-pity, bitterness, hatred, and the lie that their lives, stories, and sufferings have no meaning. Instead, they choose faith, gratitude, service, hope, and love.

> They choose a lifestyle of appreciation and develop the habit of gratitude for even the simplest things—things that they'd been deprived of in their seasons of terror, such as water, food, conversation, companionship, comfort, and laughter.

> They refuse to let the atrocities that scarred them and stripped them of their dignity, their loved ones, and everything they owned steal the Shine inside them.

> They choose to believe that there was a good reason they survived, and they decide to become and remain a part of the good and light in this world.

Their stories taught me that no matter how much my heart was aching or what or who caused the ache, I can always choose gratitude, kindness, and hope. And I believe you can too. The Bible calls Jesus' followers "the light of the world"[5] and "children of the light."[6] Jesus has also told His followers, "In this world you will have trouble. But take heart! I have overcome the world."[7]

This is how you overcome: On a moment-by-moment basis, you decide you will be the one to light a candle instead of cursing the darkness. Maybe this is the choice you're facing right now. The rest of your life depends on what you decide to believe about what you're capable of, your worth, and the meaning of your life.

From now on, please remember that you can always choose what you will focus on and move toward. There are really only two options:

> more bitterness, more sadness, more isolation, more anger

or

> tiny, courageous steps toward freedom, peace,
  and—eventually—joy

And I do mean *tiny*. In fact, the tinier, the better. Human beings were designed to grow through baby steps. These are the incremental choices that last, and they're the only way to literally reprogram your mind out of the darkness of sorrow.

We Need You to Hope Again

Committing to wellness and growth is not saying that what happened to you was okay.

Of course it wasn't okay, and nothing will make it right.

But you survived. You're here, right now, and that's something to celebrate.

You're here for a good reason. The unique expression of love and light only you are capable of, the hope you bring, and the gifts you share are priceless.

One of my favorite scenes in the movie *X-Men: Days of Future Past* is when young Charles Xavier travels forward in time fifty years to have a conversation with the older version of himself. Sunlight streams through stained glass as young Charles leans toward Professor X, locking eyes with his future self. Charles's heart has been completely crushed. He's overwhelmed by the evil that has claimed the lives of his family, and he's ashamed of not being strong enough to gain victory over his sorrow. To numb his pain, he's turned to drugs.

Professor X then gifts him with a glimpse of his future: halls filled with hopeful, encouraged students at Xavier's School for Gifted Youngsters. Hundreds of children who were abused, devalued, and abandoned are now safely living in a place where they can learn to discover, control, and use their gifts for good in the world.

Professor X then explains, "Just because someone stumbles, loses their way—it doesn't mean they're lost forever. Sometimes we all need a little help. . . . We need you to hope again."[8]

So here you are. Just as Charles was in the movie, you are facing a pivotal moment in your life, my friend. This is a plot-twist scene in your story: You've been given a chance to choose hope again. And the decision you make now will change everything that happens in the next moment. Choose your next thought strategically, and always and only be kind—to others and to yourself.

What's Your Mission?

How would you describe yourself today? What kind of person are you? What kind of person would you most like to become? Whom do you admire? What characters in your favorite stories do you long to be more like? What is your personal definition of success and abundance?

Do you remember the promise I made as a twelve-year-old at Dachau? I decided that somehow, some way, I would be a part of the good in this world. That promise shaped every decision I made after leaving the concentration camp. In a way, it gave me an objective to focus on and a mission to be a part of.

On a small level, I understood that although many things were completely out of my control, I could control the direction of my life and make choices to become the kind of person I most wanted to be. This is one of the most beautiful things about being human: We can move forward in the directions we choose as we design the life we feel we most deserve.

One of the most important truths I pray you'll discover is that God is not concerned about your accomplishments. He is most concerned with the kind of person you are becoming.

Jesus is described as "a man of sorrows . . . acquainted with grief,"[9] but He was also on mission. The Scriptures explain that "for the joy set before him he endured the cross."[10] The joy set before Him? What happened to Him wasn't fair. It wasn't right. But God did it for love—love for you and me and everyone who dares to believe and wants to come home for good.

So what's your mission? To allow sorrow and sadness to suffocate your light? Or will you choose to Shine, one tiny choice at a time? All the things that have happened to cause you to forget your worth will fall away, one by one, every single tiny time you choose the path of faith, hope, gratitude, and joy.

I'm so excited and honored that you've chosen to travel with me this far as we keep moving forward in this healing journey.

TinyHabit #4: Tiny Mission Statements

With every TinyHabit you create to customize your wellness strategy, you make an important contribution toward good in humanity's story. And TinyHabits make it easier to be in the moment—where God is—rather than spinning off into memory or fantasizing about the future—where no one is.

As you choose the next good, right, and healthy thing, you become a partner in God's good work.

Today I invite you to create a simplified Tiny Mission Statement. Be sure to make it specific and concrete—something you can take action toward immediately.

Here are some examples:

Tiny Mission Statement (Anchor)	Possible TinyHabit (Behavior)
I am an encourager, therefore . . .	I will send a message of encouragement to at least one friend, family member, or coworker today.
I am thankful, therefore . . .	I will leave a sticky note on my spouse's dashboard today that says, "I appreciate you very much."
I am a helper, therefore . . .	I will ask someone close to me how I might help out with one of their tasks today.
I am joyful, therefore . . .	I will smile at a stranger at least once today.
I am loving, therefore . . .	I will say, "I'm so happy to see you!" when I see my children after school.
I am creative, therefore . . .	I will make something today—anything!
I am faithful, therefore . . .	I will read one line of Scripture today.

And, as always, remember to celebrate after you take action. Tiny Celebrations create Shine and literally wire the new habit into your brain.

To remember your Tiny Mission Statement until it becomes a habit, consider trying some of these ideas:

> Print it out and tape it to your bathroom mirror.

> Write it on several sticky notes. Put one in every room and in the car. The insides of kitchen cabinets and inside the fridge are also fun.

> Make it the wallpaper on your phone or laptop.

> Tell Alexa, Siri, Google Home, or Cortana to remind you to say it out loud at scheduled times throughout the day.

> Tape the printed statement to the ceiling in your bedroom (if you sleep on your back—tape it on the wall if you're a side sleeper).

> Write it on your hand with a Sharpie. (I love this one!)

You get the idea, right? These are things I did because I was on a mission for wellness—body, mind, spirit, and soul. I'd also include a supporting Scripture reference, because part of my mission was to get to know God better.

Here is a sample TinyHabit recipe that includes the Tiny Mission Statement:

Anchor: After I see my sticky note . . .

Tiny Behavior: I will say, out loud, "I am joyful" (Psalm 16:11).

Celebration and Shine: Then I will lift my chin, take a deep, calming breath, and smile toward the heavens.

Creating a Tiny Mission Statement is fun! You'll probably surprise yourself as you walk it out each day, and you'll surprise your loved ones as well. They may even ask to join you, which would be awesome—one of the best ways to learn is to teach. So go ahead, have fun, and get ready to grow—for good!

Chapter 5

TAKE COURAGE AND SLOW DOWN

A Master Plan

It's not a sin to have a broken heart.

PASTOR BOB MOELLER

WE LIVE AT THE SPEED OF LIGHT. It's a bit insane to witness after you've returned from spending time in a culture where things are nowhere near as urgent as everything seems here in the United States.

We're often so busy being busy that we may feel a little ashamed if someone asks how we're doing and we haven't done anything lately that's worthy of a selfie or a social media post.

Busyness is the drug of choice for many people who are trying to cope with sorrow.

For too many years it was one of mine—busyness . . . and Baskin-Robbins bubblegum or cookie dough ice cream.

When my mother died in 2015, I had recently returned from a service trip to Mongolia, and I was extremely busy hosting a major-market morning radio show. I was working overtime and recovering from a dangerous bacterial infection in my blood. Still,

I never slowed down long enough to fully heal. I was headed to the doctor again with a fever when I received the text from my sister telling me that Mama had died. Even still, I didn't slow down.

I know now that I was using busyness to numb my pain and to try to outrun my sorrow. My relationship with my mother had been very complicated, confusing, and deeply painful. Her death changed that relationship in ways I wasn't ready for. To be honest, I also felt guilty for feeling relieved by it.

She was very sick. She was terrorized by mental illness and very unhappy for as long as I knew her. Her death meant that for the first time in my life, I had to accept that there really was nothing I could do to help her. The war was finally over, and all that remained of her was sadness, as my six siblings and I wondered what might have been, if only . . .

Because I didn't want to deal with all the entangled, difficult feelings, I got even busier. I lied to myself every day, saying that I simply didn't have time and that there were too many "good" things to get done that were much more important than taking the time to work through my emotions.

Then one day, the vice president of broadcasting walked over to my desk and asked, "Do you know that you can take all the time you need to recover?" I thanked him, told him I was fine, and continued at my regular pace.

It was around that time that I interviewed an author who challenged and changed my life with one sentence: She said, quite simply, "It takes courage to slow down."

This cut me to my core. I hadn't considered that busyness is often the firstborn child of fear and that all my "good" work was really a façade.

Deep down, I was afraid. I hardly slept. I gained fifteen pounds. One afternoon, I left a post-show meeting and drove straight to the ER, dizzy and completely exhausted.

As I slowly recovered, I heard God telling me that busyness is actually a cheap imitation of life. It produces false hope and a shallow existence. The more you and I choose constant activity over loving self-care, the more we lose and betray ourselves.

Grieving on Purpose

Grief is work. When you intentionally slow down to grieve the losses created by trauma, you gain the opportunity to see and acknowledge the root causes of many of your emotional and physiological reactions and responses.

If you take the time—even if it's only a few minutes each day—to intentionally identify and process the root issues causing your heartache, depression, and exhaustion, you'll incrementally begin to feel empowered. Taking courage and slowing down afford you the time you need to begin and continue in your healing journey.

The core reason that you can't outrun sadness is because, as Pastor Bob Moeller once told me, "Sorrow is a gift." It's a gift with a purpose: As with the pain of a broken bone, the deep pain in your heart and spirit enables you to acknowledge and understand that you've been wounded. Therefore, logically, you must make time to get the help and support you need to heal.

Sorrow is a signal that it's time to slow down. It's an invitation to stop running and to rest and grieve your losses so that healing and recovery can begin and progress.

I call this *grieving on purpose*. Slowing down helped me see that I already had the tools I needed for wellness. I discovered that God had answered my prayers by leading me to become an expert in Behavior Design.

In a moment of crystal clarity, I combined the models and methods of Behavior Design and TinyHabits into a personalized *behavior-change Master Plan*.[1] The plan is effective because it's built on how human behavior actually works.

As a Behavior Designer, I'm blessed to teach the *Fogg Behavior Model*, which I believe to be a theory equivalent to $E=mc^2$ in terms of both simplicity and importance. It's surprisingly simple, because there are only three variables that drive every human behavior. Behavior happens when three elements come together at the same moment: motivation, ability, and a prompt.

The model looks like this:

B = MAP

or

behavior = motivation, ability, prompt

When the convergence happens, the behavior occurs. The *motivation* is the fact that you already want to do this behavior to accomplish a specific outcome. *Ability* is your capacity to perform the specific behavior. The *prompt* is the thing that says, "Do this" or "Take action now."

The prompt is like a notification that pops up on your phone. If you receive a prompt and you're motivated and able to take action, the behavior will occur.

You're reading this book, and you're in pretty deep at this point, so you're definitely motivated to take action to be well and move forward from the pervasive sadness. This is something you already want to do, which means you have built-in motivation.

It's very likely that since you've chosen to read this book on trauma recovery, the prompt for choosing it as a resource was the emotion of sadness and sorrow. This is why I'm sharing the Behavior Model.

As trauma survivors, we live daily with a very undesirable, continual prompt: that feeling of sorrow and sadness. The Behavior Model allows us to see how the negative feeling (motivation) is actually a helpful prompt that we can use as the anchor to design a good Tiny Behavior.

This gives us back control. And it's not a false sense of control—it's real and powerful.

Let me explain using a common example:

Behavior: staying in bed
Motivation: believing life is worthless (i.e., *What's the use?*—we're all motivated by our beliefs.)
Ability: lying there
Prompt: sadness, depression, sorrow

If you reframe your ideas about what the emotions of sadness and sorrow really mean and understand that these painful feelings are actually a prompt to take action, then suddenly they become a helpful tool toward recovery. *You're sad because you're wounded and in need of loving care.*

Please consider the following first starts to a new day:

Option 1: "I'm feeling sad again. What's wrong with me? My life is worthless—I'll never feel any better. I'm going to stay in bed."

Option 2: "I'm feeling sad again, and this is a prompt to take action! I'll use my TinyHabit and say out loud, 'It's going to be a great day—somehow.' Then I'll smile to celebrate and create Shine."

Notice how different these first starts are for the day. Which option moves you closer to being the person you want to be?

Which tiny mindset will help you feel successful enough to take the next step and do the next right thing?

In matters of recovery, you must decide that you will deliberately and strategically choose kind thoughts, behaviors, and responses to every prompt—because you're prompted hundreds of times a day.

As an example, let's say a coworker at the morning meeting wants attention and makes a comment about you arriving late. You suddenly feel ashamed and devalued, disappointed with yourself and life. But you now know that those feelings are a prompt related to deeper pain. You recognize the feelings, take a deep, quick breath, and respond, "Thanks for pointing that out. I did it to make you look good!" And then smile. (Yes, I know that may be a little passive-aggressive, but it will get the other person thinking and allow you to hold your ground.)

One of my favorite Scriptures about this suggests that in spite of the circumstances God can enable and equip us to offer up a "sacrifice of praise."[2] God knows that choosing what's good and right, such as praise, is not always easy—it may even feel impossible—but He always enables the willing. "Whatever is true, whatever is noble, whatever is right, whatever is pure, whatever is lovely, whatever is admirable—if anything is excellent or praiseworthy—think about such things."[3] And His peace and power will be with us as we go.

If you choose to reframe and redefine your sadness as a prompt to choose specific good and healthy actions, your life will incrementally begin to change for good.

Be patient and consistent in this process, and you will succeed.

If you do make it out of bed, that's awesome. You may want to stand up and try out one of my favorite tiny prayers: *Jesus, please help me.* Then celebrate and create Shine by smiling and stretching both arms up high. You can even do this in a business meeting by praying in your heart with your eyes wide open, turning both palms up under the table in surrender.

It feels so great—it feels like freedom!

Focusing only on your sadness drains your life from you. But choosing a tiny but helpful behavior when that sadness prompts you and then celebrating that good decision renews your hope, strengthens your spirit, and generates courage.

Once you make the loving self-care decision to slow down and create a Master Plan for grieving on purpose, you will feel your joy increase all throughout the day.

Goals Don't Work—Systems Do

Have you ever made a New Year's resolution? Then you know how those commonly work out. Not so great, right? But there's no reason to play the guilt, shame, and self-condemnation game. These types of personal failures have nothing to do with a lack of willpower. Instead, they have everything to do with a fundamental misunderstanding of how human behavior was designed to work.

Goals are nice, but they're too vague and abstract—humans are designed to move forward incrementally and systematically toward concrete objectives. This is why, for most of us, goals don't work for sustained results.

We're culturally conditioned to believe that big leaps lead to big results. The whole go-big-or-go-home mindset is based on a flawed idea. Big leaps and motivation waves are profitable for fitness clubs, but they don't work for most individuals. Big leaps are unsustainable, but good systems and strategies built on tiny, concrete objectives will always lead to favorable outcomes.

God is a systems guy, and His design for human behavior is systematic.

That's why your personal system designed for recovery *will* work as you walk it out, seeking God's perspective on your progress, one tiny choice after the next.

Suppose you want to get rid of a bad habit, such as bingeing on ice cream (one of my former bad habits that became an addiction). Whenever you feel depressed (prompted by sadness), using the Behavior Model and TinyHabits, you can create your own systematic Master Plan that will work best for you—one tiny choice at a time.

Each TinyHabit carried out successfully leads to tiny victories and cause for everyday celebrations. I'll tell you how this has worked for me and for so many others.

A good first strategic step is choosing to slow down and make time to find out specifically what you're grieving.

Next, take action in the tiniest, simplest way you can. Break this behavior down to its smallest form. For example, when prompted by my sadness, I journaled for two to five minutes at a time. Each time my sadness showed up, I journaled specifically about that feeling.[4]

Through this tiny, strategic journaling activity, I realized in time that what I was actually looking for was nurture, provision, protection, and the sense of home I never received during my growing years.

Even the hope of that nurture was gone because my only remaining parent was gone. Realizing this was an aha moment for me that enabled me to ask myself some very important questions:

Why am I still looking for something that's impossible to find? Why am I still trying to find or earn a type of love that was never meant to be a part of my story on this side of heaven?

The tiny two- to five-minute journal entries helped me see clearly that I was looking for closure for and resolution to all the situations directly related to my chaotic, abusive childhood.

I also often do a tiny meditation with three deep breaths, which specifically helps in the alleviation of PTSD symptoms in my body and mind.[5] The breathing calms my stress response systems and reminds me that I am safe, provided for, and protected—no matter what happens, God is near and I'm going to be okay.

The system you create is customized for you. Your consistent and faithful good work will reveal many good things about you, and it won't take long for you to see the trauma-created fog clearing. Your energy will incrementally increase and your stress will decline as the pace of life slows down for you. It really does feel miraculous, because it's built on love. Making tiny, intentional, healthy self-care decisions affirms your worth and value as a person. You slowly begin to see that your needs are just as important as the needs of others.

A loving self-care system based on how human behavior actually works will help you move forward empowered and equipped to finally let the unhealthy responses to the prompt of sadness go. As you begin to live your life on purpose, your perspective and identity will begin to shift toward the light.

The TinyHabits Trauma-Recovery Tool Kit

TinyHabits invite you to see the truth that you can always take your next good step. Tiny and simple keeps you moving forward, because you always have the ability to take action and do *something*.

This is how, prompted by pain, you created the unhealthy, undesirable habits to numb your sorrow. You felt sadness and took action.

Now, using that same prompt of sadness, you can begin creating healthy habits rooted in loving self-care. But first, you need to gather the perfect tools for your recovery. I call this the *TinyHabits trauma-recovery tool kit*.

This is an actual tool kit you create. It's easily accessed and filled with resources you know will help you keep moving forward. It can be digital or physical or both, as mine is.

For a physical tool kit, I suggest a container that appeals to you: a treasure box, a decorated shoebox, a beautiful basket, or even an actual Craftsman metal toolbox. Maybe your tool kit is a trunk at the foot of your bed.

You decide what will work best. For a digital version, create a folder and call it something like "My Tool Kit" or "Inspiration and Motivation." Name it whatever you want, as long as seeing it reminds you of the importance of prioritizing your healing journey.

Just as those who use rescue inhalers for asthma carry what they need for relief and wellness, you will also have access to your tool kit whenever you need it.

The tool kit is your place to keep a collection of items that inspire and create Shine. The contents will change as you grow and heal.

Here are a few examples of things to add to your tool kit:

> TinyHabit recipes
> favorite Scriptures
> precious keepsakes
> pictures of children
> photos of friends
> mementos of favorite moments
> essential oils
> favorite childhood toys
> inspiring quotations
> encouraging affirmations
> a journal or voice recorder
> stuffed animals
> hashtags you follow
> _____
> _____
> _____

I'm sometimes asked about the essential oils in my tool kit. These are a way to smell my favorite scents every day. Essential oils have been proven to calm the nervous system. They can also serve as a multisensory reminder of how much God cares about every detail of your life. He's the One who knew you'd love that scent the moment He dreamed you up.[6]

If essential oils aren't for you, that's fine. Just be sure to add to your tool kit anything and everything that brings you a spark of joy and creates a feeling of Shine when you see or hold it. It's good to keep the physical toolbox in what I call a *sacred space* in your home—a space set aside for you to take loving self-care toward recovery.

I also highly recommend getting a journal or binder where you can write things down. Think of it as a "captain's log"—a place to record your progress, prayers, and insights along the way.

If you're not a fan of writing in journals, you can use your phone or laptop. Even a voice recorder is a good way to process and document your healing journey. On the hard days, having such a log will help you look back or listen and see just how far you've come and how much you've grown. Whether digital or physical, choose whatever journaling method is most convenient for you. And like all TinyHabit anchors, make sure it fits easily into your existing lifestyle and routine.

Remember my unhealthy sugar-habit-turned-addiction caused by the prompt of my grief and sorrow?

Every time I felt prompted by my sadness, I would make time in my schedule and budget for bubblegum or cookie dough ice cream. I'd then justify my unhealthy decision and tell myself that I was too busy to eat right—that I'd work on it some other time.

After I created my Master Plan with Behavior Design and TinyHabits, when prompted by sorrow, I'd grab my journal and make a quick note. I would often do this during songs or commercial breaks when I was hosting my radio show. I always wrote something tiny but good.

In other contexts, I would get my essential oil from my tiny tool kit (a scaled-down version in my purse) and take two quick, deep breaths. I then celebrated that decision in a tiny, healthy, loving way to create and enjoy Shine.

Your strategy and tool kit should be perfectly tailored to you and your personal situational contexts. I suggest keeping a tool kit at home and a tiny tool kit for portability.

To look at it another way: We don't find it unusual for people to carry their prescriptions with them. Your TinyHabits trauma-recovery tool kit is just as important—perhaps even more so, because TinyHabits shift your perspective toward good (even your perspective on any physical illnesses you may have).

My prayer is that we will shift as a culture to understanding that mental health is a key component of physical health. Recovery is not an optional afterthought, just as resetting a broken or dis-jointed bone should never be an optional afterthought. I mean, how can you and I justify being angry about abuse and injustice if we continue to engage in abusive, unhealthy, and unloving behaviors toward ourselves?

Please remember to be gracious and kind to yourself, because there will be some trial and error as you learn what works for you. Journaling or voice memos may not be your thing, but think about what *will* effectively remind you to keep moving forward in your healing journey.

No one has more influence on you than you. What tiny choice

can you make right now to create space and discover what you need? What Master Plan will you create to grieve your losses and keep moving forward?

The Superpower of Celebration

Now that you've chosen to create your own TinyHabits Master Plan for moving forward, it's time to spend more time mastering the transforming skill of Celebration, which produces the feeling of Shine. You must master this skill because it produces bursts of dopamine—the happiness hormone—throughout your day.

If you've ever spent time taking care of a baby, you know that in a loving, healthy home, celebrating tiny victories all throughout the day is simply how it's done. Just by showing up, new babies move healthy parents and caretakers into the realm of continual Tiny Celebrations and Shine.

As soon as that baby first opens his eyes in the hospital room, he blinks and cries, trying to adjust to all those bright lights. He shivers in shock from the cold, and he is startled by the volume and chaos created by his arrival here on planet Earth!

He's crying too hard to see that there's actually a celebration going on. Joy abounds, as every one of the giants who make up the welcoming committee in the room are thrilled to greet him! They've been waiting so long!

Everyone rejoices, the phones come out, and the picture taking doesn't stop!

And all the baby did was open his eyes and cry.

Please think about this with me: Close your eyes and imagine the moment of a baby's arrival. This can help you understand what God's love for you is really like.

> When a baby first latches onto her mother's breast for nursing—Tiny Celebration and Shine!
> He lifts his head all by himself—Tiny Celebration and Shine!
> She rolls over—Tiny Celebration and Shine!
> He holds the bottle all on his own—Tiny Celebration and Shine!
> She takes her first steps—Tiny Celebration and Shine!
> He uses the potty for the first time—Tiny Celebration and Shine!
> She grows a tooth without even trying—Tiny Celebration and Shine!

For babies in healthy families with healthy caretakers, life is filled with tiny milestones, tiny victories, Tiny Celebrations, and wonder-filled days overflowing with Shine! Celebration is a fundamental part of God's design for humanity. Celebration bonds us together and inspires us to create and maintain long-term relational connections. Consider the way celebrations are at the heart of all our community, covenant, team, and fellowship experiences. They are as important to humanity as air, food, and water.

This is why daily celebrations of our babies' tiny accomplishments bring joy and encourage them to keep moving forward. Many of their accomplishments have nothing to do with their efforts. We cheer when they grow new teeth or smile. Babies begin to understand real love through celebration and affirmation of their value in this world.

As we grow, we are taught how to celebrate in healthy or unhealthy ways. The results of these decisions always manifest as we watch our choices accumulate into a lifetime and legacy.

This is why things often go so wrong when the celebrations suddenly stop. Children know immediately when we're no longer happy to see them, and they respond accordingly. For some, the shock is so confusing and devastating that it sets off decades of unhealthy decisions.

When we stop loving someone simply for who they are, they notice. Many adults can vividly recall a time in their lives when things shifted from celebration to disappointment in a relationship with a caretaker or parent. But no matter how far we may wander into the darkness of that disappointment, there's always hope.

Tiny Celebrations and the feelings of Shine they produce can lead to opportunities for you to discover your true potential. This is what all healthy, loving parents want for their children—and God is the perfect parent. The fact that we begin this journey as helpless babies is not an accident or a design flaw. We were made for love by Love,[7] and true love is filled with Tiny Celebrations.

Fun, Free, and Easy!

One of the most important and powerful maxims of Behavior Design is "Help people feel successful." This is one of the ways we help innovators design products, systems, and services that work for good all over the world in every cultural context. When people feel successful, they stay motivated and often come back for more.

The decision to master the habit of Tiny Celebrations will be one of the best choices you'll ever make—it will equip you with simple tools to satisfy this need for yourself. And maybe the best part of all is that Tiny Celebrations are fun, free, and easy!

Most recovery programs offer effective, built-in Tiny Celebrations. For example, receiving a twelve-step-recovery medallion or a Celebrate Recovery coin is a joy-filled, deeply personal moment of connection for many who are serious about the healing journey.

As you create and succeed with your TinyHabits, you will feel empowered to take the next tiny step toward sustained joy. My Behavior Design mentor, Dr. B. J. Fogg, taught me that habits are like seeds. Start small, find the right place for them, and grow them over time.

Jesus explained in one of my favorite parables that it's God who provides good seeds. He invites us to receive and sow seeds of love. He does this so our lives will produce good results that help others know what He is like.

But depending on the type of soil you are, there may or may not be a good harvest to come. He described some of our soil as rocky, shallow, and hardened. Sometimes we're too busy with worries and too set in our sorrow and self-pity to receive His life-giving seeds and living water.[8]

In many ways, this parable is like a blueprint you can use as a foundation for building your trauma-recovery Master Plan. Start by asking the following question: *What kind of soil do I most want to be?*

If it's good soil, as Jesus says, you'll need to slow down to begin cultivating a heart and soul that courageously faces, accepts, and grieves your losses, heartaches, and regrets in healthy ways. Then you will feel empowered to move toward becoming someone who is in the habit of making healing choices—someone who finds and celebrates what's good, the person in the room who remains fully present and thankful.

Well done! You have read to the end of chapter 5 in a book about moving forward! Now is the perfect time for a Tiny Celebration! Maybe stand up, raise your hands to heaven, smile big, and say, "I'm awesome!"

Go ahead and celebrate this fine and courageous work you've done to slow down and take this tiny step toward joy.

TinyHabit #5: Mastering the Art of Tiny Celebrations

Do you like the person you're on this journey with? Not the person who might be on your last nerve today, but the person who greets you in the mirror every morning?

I hope so. Liking yourself and learning to really love yourself is healthy, and it's the best way to stay fully present and truly thankful in your journey.

There are few things more exhausting, discouraging, and distracting than wishing to be someone else in your own story.

The daily decision to dislike or even hate yourself is, in fact, a decision—one you can change right now, one TinyHabit and Tiny Celebration at a time.

This is why the TinyHabit for today is to learn how to celebrate in tiny, healthy ways the gift that you are in this world.

Always remember the TinyHabit formula:

ABC: Anchor, Behavior, Celebration

> Anchor Moment: After I notice my reflection in the mirror . . .
> Tiny Behavior: I will say out loud, "Hello there! I'm happy to see you!"
> Celebration and Shine: Then I will smile and say out loud, "Looking good!"

This is one of the best TinyHabit recipes I know to move you toward mastery of the art of Tiny Celebrations. Here's another of my personal favorites:

> Anchor Moment: After I brush my teeth,
> Tiny Behavior: I will say out loud, "Thank You, God— You're with me, and it's going to be a great day!"
> Celebration and Shine: Then I will smile and take a slow, deep breath—in through my nose, out through my mouth.

Below are a few of my favorite tiny ways to celebrate and wire into my brain a new TinyHabit toward recovery. These are just a few—there are hundreds and even thousands more!

> Do a quick fist pump and say, *Thank You, God!*
> Smile and give yourself a hug.
> Raise your arms and say, *Today is a day of victory!*
> Turn both palms up and say, *Praise You, Lord!*
> Say to yourself, *I got this, and I'm never alone.*
> Smile and do a happy dance (sitting or standing).
> Take a deep breath, smile, and put your palms together in gratitude.
> Lift your head high and smile.
> Smile and say, *Well done.*
> Recruit a child to do a quick happy dance with you. (The younger the better, because they're experts at Tiny Celebration happy dances.)
> _____
> _____
> _____

These are just a few examples—you'll want to come up with the healthy Tiny Celebrations that work best for you.

Notice how several of the celebrations include smiling. One of my favorite studies on depression recovery focused completely on the power of intentional smiling for set periods of time.[9] Even participants suffering from severe depression showed improvements when they simply smiled and were silly in the mirror for set times every day.

Don't worry if you don't get it right on the first try. Always celebrate every attempt. Yes, it's a participation award, but this practice is powerful when done right.

As I always told my coding students, don't ever give up—keep on designing toward victory.

Please don't ever forget the transformative power of Tiny Celebrations and Shine.

Love and encourage that amazing little child inside you who's longing to be celebrated the way that you've always deserved.

You are a wonder-filled and beautiful gift from God in a world desperately in need of the one-of-a-kind Shine only you can bring!

I'm happy from the inside out.

PSALM 16:9, *MSG*

Chapter 6

LEARN YOUR GIFTS AND TRUST YOUR ALLIES

Finding Strength and Accepting Support

Your mind and emotions are gifts—two of many. Identifying and using your gifts invites healing and enables you to break through the fears keeping you from the healthy relationships you were created to enjoy.

SOME TIME AGO, when I was working through a particularly dark and desperate season of sorrow, I read a curious teaching on depression and sadness that reminded me of a sci-fi movie, complete with an evil-alien-invasion plotline. It went something like this: When the feelings of sorrow and sadness show up in your life, it's because deep inside you is an evil, dark, parasitic entity that feeds on pain, negativity, and self-pity. Every time you're triggered by a situation, this dark entity awakens within you. It rises up and tries to overpower you, take you down, and keep you there so it can take over your life.

As it controls your reactions and responses, it also urges you to unite with others who are controlled by its darkness. It keeps you up at night, reminding you of all your worst experiences and mistakes. The author of this theory believes that when the dark entity is in control, you'll want to create more pain by harming yourself and allowing your hurt to overflow onto others.

As I said, it reads like a sci-fi alien-invasion plot!

In my desperation at the time, this strange yet intriguing theory made a lot of sense to me. I've seen that painful scenario played out up close and personal in many people's lives. I've seen firsthand the way that if you allow the darkness to rule and control you, you become a source of pain for others. Many people become just like their abusers: sources of suffering, chaos, confusion, and pain. And they often justify their choices by saying that they're sorry but it's all they know how to do.

Thankfully, the author of the sci-fi soul-invader theory (as I call it) didn't just leave the reader with questions—he also offered a strategy to defeat the dark entity. According to the author, in order to defeat the invader and be free, you need to cultivate and master the art of embracing the present moment. As soon as you embrace it, the entity begins to "dissolve," and you can go on with your day.

I get it. I understand exactly why this concept is so popular. It's really enticing when you just want the emotional pain to stop. Honestly, that's exactly why I bought the book—I just wanted the emotional pain to stop.

But the danger lies in the fact that in order to continue to defeat or "dissolve" the evil, destructive entity, you have to make an enemy of two of the greatest gifts God has given you: your mind and emotions. Consider the following:

> Your circulatory system processes and circulates your blood.
> Your respiratory system processes and exhales air.
> Your digestive system absorbs nutrients and digests food.
> Your nervous system—including your mind and emotions—prompts and enables you to process data, respond, and react.

Your mind and your emotions are parts of a loving and practical God-given system. They're not enemies—they're gifts with specific purposes and functions.

> Your thoughts create your emotions.
> Your emotions create your habits.
> Your habits create your life.[1]

Teachings similar to the one I described above seem to disregard the fact that people don't choose the traumatic circumstances and mental illnesses caused by abuse, neglect, poverty, and trauma. The sadness, thoughts, and feelings caused by these traumatic experiences are *normal*, healthy, human responses to injustice and evil.

When your mind and emotions are doing their jobs as they are designed, you can make a tiny, healthy choice every time the reminder of that unprocessed, unhealed pain arises. I know it hurts and is very difficult to manage, but just as quickly as you can make a tiny, unhealthy choice you can instead make a healthy and healing choice. Most of us can succeed in this if we really want to.[2]

It's loving and wise to acknowledge your pain and honor what you're experiencing and feeling. It's unloving and unhealthy to try to distract yourself from that pain by focusing only on the good things in the present moment. Gratitude is important, but adopting the bad habit of forced optimism is unhealthy. You have the right to feel and process what you're feeling. If your leg is broken, you need rest and loving care—not a 5K to run.

If you choose to suppress, dissolve, or ignore the pain, it's only going to come back—over and over again until you address the core issues. Your mind and emotions are not enemies that awaken and rise up to steal your joy and take over your life. They are gifts given to serve and accomplish specific purposes for your good.

Without attending to your mind (and the emotions it generates) there's no real life—just a numbed-out, autopilot version. This kind of life is dependent on and driven by desires and impulses. And it is completely cut off from opportunities to feel and be fully present so you can notice, appreciate, and enjoy the good things and people in your life. If we don't engage with our minds and emotions, we become like broken machines permanently programmed to produce mundane, negative outcomes with frustrating, insanely repetitive results.

New Systems, New Thoughts, and New Habits

Systems design is both an art and a science. I mentioned this in chapter 1, and here's a bit of a refresher: In programming, every keystroke, space, and symbol that makes up each line of code is necessary for the program to run efficiently and expertly. *Trauma is bad code.* Your mind has created strings of thoughts and responses in order to survive.

These thoughts lead to behaviors that run like a bad program along familiar paths, generated by thousands of triggers embedded in your everyday life. Therefore, when your mind alerts you to something deep within you that needs healing and attention, this is cause for *appreciation*—not avoidance, attack, or fear. If you distract yourself from your pain, you aren't addressing the root of the problem that prompted the painful emotion and memory.

To move forward toward sustained wellness, you must focus on the root cause of the pain as soon as possible. Use the pain as a prompt to make a tiny, specific healing choice. At the very least, acknowledge that your mind is alerting you to something that needs attention by making important connections between the present situation and something much deeper.

That pain is your opportunity to discover a deeper, hidden place within yourself that's in need of loving attention and care. It's an opportunity to honor what you're feeling and make a tiny, healing choice, such as journaling about the incident that stirred up the pain and praying for wisdom and help. Please remember that if you ignore or suppress the feeling, it will surely return the very next time you're prompted, and often with greater intensity, as that wounded part of you cries out for healing, acknowledgment, and loving care.

As I write this, I'm reminded of how Jesus explained what happens when a room is swept clean of demonic influence only at a surface level. He said that seven more dark spirits will return, each one more fearsome and powerful than the previous.[3] In these passages and others, Jesus makes it clear that the spiritual war against the darkness is real. Therefore, He has equipped each of us with the ability to choose our responses and beliefs. And what we believe changes everything about how we respond.

The power and ability you have to overcome the pain caused by abuse of any and every kind is right there for you to receive every day.[4] The light is not at the end of the tunnel—Jesus is right there with you, always. You absolutely can create new systems, new strings of thought, and new habits prompted by the very feelings you most want to heal. The feelings you're tempted to numb out or suppress are actually helpful in your healing journey because they alert you to the places and spaces within you that most need your attention.

Instead of making an enemy out of your mind and the way it operates, decide today that from now on, when prompted, you will slow down and stop as soon as possible to acknowledge and appreciate the message that your mind and emotions are sending you.

One of my favorite TinyHabits for victory when I'm triggered is to choose to be thankful that my mind and emotions are doing exactly what God designed them to do—for my good.

For example, I frequently use a specific TinyHabit. When prompted by my pain, I immediately say the following out loud or quietly within:

"God, thank You for this reminder to slow down and take care."

Then I celebrate by smiling and taking a deep, slow, and mindful breath.

I always have my journal—digital or physical—with me, and I make a note as soon as possible, including the date, time, and trigger, so I can be sure to pray, learn from, and process the experience with God's help at the first opportunity to do so.

Taking Care

If you accidentally cut your finger, you can make the choice to slow down and lovingly tend to the injury so you don't bleed all over the place and so it doesn't get infected. This simple analogy demonstrates how a sequential system and strategy always helps in the healing of our wounds:

Prompt: You cut your finger. It's deep, it hurts, and it's bleeding.
1. Apply pressure to the cut.
2. Clean the wound.
3. Apply ointment.
4. Apply a bandage.
5. Be careful with the wounded area, and be patient while it heals.

Physical injuries hurt until they're fully healed—there's nothing we can do to rush the process. Unfortunately, time does not heal emotional wounds. You must move forward both cautiously, continually tending to your injuries, and victoriously, celebrating every tiny moment you succeed in choosing a healthy response.

Some of my favorite Scriptures explain that God is close to and heals the brokenhearted, binding up our wounds.[5] Binding is a process—it takes time and careful, loving attention. Just as an injury to the body requires physical therapy, emotional healing also requires therapy, time, and careful, repeated practice in order to build strength back into broken and disjointed places.

Even if the healing journey takes a lifetime, it's not fair, but you must still be loving, patient, systematic, and intentional. Remember that life is a process and a journey. And because this world in its present state is not as it will be, we are all on healing journeys. You are never alone.

Please don't be angry with yourself or with God for your ability to feel pain. Just commit to taking the time to attend to your wounds. Even when you feel angry with God, it's okay. Always express in prayer exactly how you feel. Don't try to dress it up and make it formal and proper. And please don't worry— He's God. He made the multiverse! He can definitely handle your anger.

The One who designed your mind is good. He loves you and longs for you to move into alignment with His will for your life: You are to become and remain a source of His goodness, righteousness, love, and light. As Scripture says, you are to be "conformed to the image of his Son."[6]

If you distract yourself or numb out, you'll forget to tend to your injury, only to find yourself constantly triggered. And that will lead to a miserable existence. But if you listen to the message your mind and emotions are trying to tell you, you'll honor yourself and your story and be able to address the root of your sorrow. Only then will you begin to heal, because love and truth always invite healing—even when it hurts.

Finding Your Gifts in Sacred Spaces

How is your personal space these days?

I'm not talking about how close you sit to strangers. This is about *having* a personal space. No matter how small your home is, I encourage you to look around and strategically designate at least one sacred space where you can focus on finding your gifts and resting in the uninterrupted presence of God.

We all need a personal place that's set apart and sacred—it's part of our human desire for home.

Many people who are interested in quickly acquiring a second language will move to another country to successfully speed things up. This is because environmental immersion is a great way to accelerate the acquisition of new languages and skills.

When it comes to becoming a master "TinyHabiteer"[7] who is fluent in tiny systems that work for good, sacred spaces are where you can be alone to focus, regroup, and recover from the stress of the day.

When my family was living in a small, two-bedroom apartment with no room indoors for a sacred space, I bought a pop-up tent and put it on the back porch. At the end of a long, stressful day that began at 3:35 every morning and was followed by hours of hosting live radio, the tent was my space—sometimes even when it snowed. I'd go inside, zip it up tightly, and review my two- to five-minute journal entries. I would reread my favorite Scriptures out loud and talk with God. The strength, insights, healing, and growth that happened in that tent were miraculous.

If you have younger children, they might be immediately drawn to your sacred space—and that's great! Finding them there is a Shine opportunity—it gives you a chance to talk with them about the importance of sacred spaces for resting your mind and meeting with God.

You are an amazing, miraculous person with an eternal destiny. You deserve a space that's all your own—a place to meet with God. No matter the square footage, it's important that it's set apart just for you so that when you arrive there, your mind, soul, spirit, and body know that it's time to be still.

The choice to be quiet and still—even if it's for just a couple of minutes—is a transcendent decision. When you are in the habit of being still, you gain the opportunity to discover life's greatest gifts. Courage and strength are gifts, love and gratitude are gifts, hope and grace are gifts, creativity is a gift, and faith is a gift—all of them from God because of love.

When you accept these gifts with heartfelt appreciation, new doors will open for you, and you'll feel empowered to keep moving forward. Your sacred space is the place where you can go to make time to enjoy these gifts. It's also a place to be deliberately creative and kind to yourself each day—creative with your prayers and creative with your favorite artistic expressions and helpful thoughts. Paint or sketch a picture, write a poem, dismantle and rebuild a gadget, make some music, do that thing you loved as a child before your innocence was stolen and your personal space was violated and disrespected. *Take it all back today*—rewrite your story as the strong, determined, victorious survivor you are.

These sacred places and times in your day allow you to come up with fresh ideas and find renewal for your spirit as you process and gather the lessons and celebrate the blessings of the day. It's also a great spot to make a strong start in the morning!

Yes, I'm inviting you to take a strategic, intentional time-out. And not because you're in trouble, but because you are so loved.

Taking a Relationship Inventory

One of my favorite proverbs explains that if you isolate yourself, you're choosing an unwise, unhealthy path, and "rag[ing] against all wise judgment."[8] I'm bringing this up because it's very common for trauma survivors to isolate themselves, believing that it will protect them from further pain—which couldn't be further from the truth.

Even still, if you've been isolating because of trauma, please don't beat yourself up. It makes sense after what you've been through. But please take the next tiny step forward by choosing to believe that there are safe people in the world.

There are people who understand. Professional trauma therapists are committed to your wellness, and truly loving people will not judge or criticize you for being wounded. There are safe people in this world who will not take advantage of you when you courageously share your pain with them. You may not have met these kinds of people yet because of the temptation to isolate. But the truth is that the resources, companions, and allies you need to recover are available.

As you begin this courageous journey away from isolation, please remember to be wise about whom you trust with your story. Be cautious of trusting people simply because of their titles. It will take some careful and diligent work to find the individuals who will make the best allies in your healing journey.

Start with prayer. Then keep reading to learn some proven tips for recognizing safe people, and begin to create your personalized plan for learning how to find these allies.

This can all be very overwhelming at first, so remember to keep your steps tiny. *Learning to trust again will take time, but you are always worth the work.*

This part of the journey begins with taking a brave inventory of the people in your life today. Who is helpful, kind, and loving? And who is harmful, self-centered, toxic, and exhausting? Years ago, when I was learning this skill, my therapist helped me make a chart. One column was for allies, and the other was for the toxic people in my life.

Allies: Who is it that when you're with them, you depart feeling braver, happier, and more equipped to deal with the stressors in your life? Who notices and celebrates your gifts and contributions—even when there's no direct benefit for them? Who shows love for you in helpful ways, and who is sincerely glad when you're doing well?

Toxic: Who drains your energy? Who encourages you to participate in activities you always or often regret? Who is critical, negative, and quick to point out what's wrong? Who takes advantage of you when you are trying to connect and be kind? Who isn't happy when you succeed, and sometimes even expresses jealously when you win an award or make personal changes for good? These are the people in your life who leave you feeling used up and unappreciated.

Taking this kind of relational inventory is courageous and healthy—though it is hard and often heartbreaking work. When you've identified people who fit into the second group—the toxic group—you make a loving choice for *both* of you when you decide to create space between you and their unhealthy behaviors. This is the space you need in order to get to know God and yourself—and to heal.

To refine the inventory, become a quiet observer. Examine the impact the people you interact with are having not only on your life but also in their personal lives and in the lives of others they encounter. What types of legacies are they leaving each day? How do others feel when they enter the room? Do they bring an atmosphere of hope, community, love, and growth with them? Or do they bring negativity and pain?

If it's the latter, I pray you'll do yourself a favor and never give them the benefit of the doubt at your own expense. There is only one Savior—and it's not you. As Maya Angelou has said, when people reveal to you what they're really about and show you who they are by being hurtful and unkind, it's wise, healthy, and respectful to believe them the very first time.[9]

With the wisdom you gain from the inventory, you can create a system that creates space so you can get out of each other's way and find healing. An individual's response to you when you tell them you are in need of more personal time will reveal which category they belong in. If they keep on calling or texting because it's always an "emergency," you don't have to answer—you are not 911 or Jesus.

One of the best things you can do if you're in a toxic relationship is leave. Get out of the way so you aren't blocking each other's views of God and what only He can do.

Negative, toxic, self-centered, and energy-depleting people are not going to help you move forward. They feel a sense of ownership, control, and entitlement over your life—even if they don't realize it. They are definitely *not* allies in your healing journey.

Finding Your Allies

Who is that person who honors and respects you enough not only to listen but also to *hear* what you have to say? They listen and care because they love you. When you spend time together, both of you feel valued and strengthened toward your purposes for good in this world.

Think of someone you admire for their genuine and consistent concern for others—someone whose faith, integrity, and inspiring ability to improve their surroundings is evident. There's a passage in the Gospels where Jesus is asked how to identify people who truly know and love God. He explains that we must always be on alert because there are deceptive people who are like "ravenous wolves," bringing lies and destruction wherever they go. He explained that a good person, like a good tree, will bring forth good fruit. In other words, take a good, strategic look at people's lives and relationships: "You will recognize them by their fruits."[10]

As you seek out allies in your healing journey, make sure you don't confide in someone you *assume* is safe. It's important to know that you can't share your story with everyone—be careful about whom you entrust with your story.

Safe people enjoy your company simply because they like you for who you are. They value your perspective and gifts, and they often notice good and helpful things about you. They appreciate your creativity, work ethic, or your attention to detail, for example. They may ask how they can help and pray with you when you're struggling. You can feel their sincere interest and compassion.

Safe people offer encouragement and expect nothing in return because their care comes from the overflow of love within them. These friends aren't interested in flattery—what matters to them is encouragement in truth, even if it's hard truth. You can tell safe people about your promotion or your kid who made the honor roll and you know they will celebrate with you from the heart.

Safe people usually have healthy, quality relationships that last over time. They won't get upset with you if you need some space to make a decision or if you don't quickly return a call or text message. They respect and encourage you to grow, and maybe even most importantly, they are sincerely and consistently kind.

These are the people who can become your allies in your healing journey, and identifying and trusting your allies can help you through your sorrow in ways you'd never expect. They are the ones you can call, text, or private message any time—because you know they want you to succeed and be well.

If someone comes to mind as you're reading this, I hope you'll reach out to tell them how much you appreciate having them in your life. Growth in the habit of expressing appreciation, no matter how tiny, makes this world a better place.

If your ally doesn't know your story because you've been holding back, maybe this could be the day that you take a brave step to share it with them over a walk or coffee. Recently a friend of mine said that it's truly a gift to allow someone to come alongside you and serve you. Many people sincerely want to help.

If you can't think of anyone right now, many churches hold Celebrate Recovery meetings on a weekly basis. There are also divorce recovery groups, grief support groups, and sexual trauma small groups. Their services are free, and these are wonderful places to meet new friends and become a part of a community that understands on a deep, heartfelt level what you're going through. Even if you just go and sit quietly in the back corner, you will grow because of that courageous healing choice.

One of the best people you can find as an ally in the healing journey is an experienced trauma therapist who understands your desire to grow in faith. I don't recommend attempting to try to move forward in healing from severe trauma without professional assistance.

My trauma therapist, Maggie, is one of the most precious people in my life. I don't know where I'd be without her or the many wonderful specialists I have met with since I was four.

This part of the process—the part where you are working on deeper pain—is more like tending a disjointed or broken bone than a deeply cut finger. It will need to be reset, cast, bound up, and then carefully retrained to gain strength with support.

Identifying and spending time with the safe people in your life is like going to the spiritual version of a physical-therapy center and trusting the technicians and physicians to help you get stronger and gain tools for healing and sustained wellness.

Joining a Celebrate Recovery or a similar specialized support group is a great place to find community with safe people. Seeing others reach their milestones, break through barriers, and celebrate can be very encouraging.

Your Most Important Ally

In the Old Testament book of Genesis, Jacob—one of the patriarchs of the faith—had an encounter with God that represents the hard work involved when learning to trust the Lord as the most important ally in your healing journey.

Jacob had quite the reputation. His very name means "deceiver." Aided and encouraged by his mother, he helped create some serious drama in his family. A betrayal he committed caused his twin brother to make a vow to murder him at the first opportunity. So Jacob ran for his life. Decades of deception and conflict followed him. It seemed that Jacob might never experience true peace. But then one night when he was alone, he finally met with God. The battle that followed was legendary, and it lasted through the night.

Jacob staggered away from the fight with a lifelong limp and a new name: Israel (which means "one who struggles or fights with God"). He also gained a brand-new understanding of the purpose for his life. He said, "I have seen God face to face, yet my life has been spared."[11] When it comes to trauma recovery and the horrors of child abuse, this description applies to you and me. God has preserved our lives for a good reason. Yet our journeys of faith will always bear the relationship status of "it's complicated."

Trauma survivors have to reconcile the realities of the problem of evil on a deeply personal level almost every day. What you believe about God's love for you is the key to overcoming and persevering through your struggle with the Almighty and the triggers that touch the wounded parts of your soul. It's the key to living out a luminous faith.

Surrendering to God's love and righteousness empowers you to keep moving forward. As my colleague and fellow neurotheologian Dr. Jim Wilder says, "Who we love has far more impact on character than what we believe."[12] Getting to know God intimately and accepting that He preserved your life for a good reason—that's the truth that Jesus said will "set you free."[13] I am living proof of this.

It's possible that I will always walk with an emotional "limp," much like Jacob after he fought with God all night. But I've decided to accept and understand that recovery of the heart, mind, and soul is a process that takes time and very hard work.

Of course I would have chosen a happier origin story for myself. But I absolutely love my life because God is the ultimate ally in the healing journey. He has taught me how to rejoice every day along the way—to dance and be happy from the inside out, even with my spiritual limp. And I've become a master at Tiny Celebrations and Shine! I pray that you will too!

I'm sorry, but there are no shortcuts. If there were, I would have found them and joyfully passed them along to you. There are no shortcuts, but there's always good news: With every good, tiny step you take, your life, relationships, self-perspective, legacy, and faith will begin to incrementally change for good. In Behavior Design, we call this proven phenomenon the *identity shift*. It's slow and incremental—but it's worth every ounce of work you put into it.

TinyHabit #6: Designing Sacred Spaces to Create Sacred Moments

Find a corner in your bedroom. Buy a pop-up tent. (Maybe put the tent in the corner of the bedroom if the weather is too cold outside.) Hang up a curtain to divide a space. Designate a bench in the backyard or under a certain tree at your favorite park. Find your sacred space and make it all your own.

Here are some of my favorite ways to create sacred spaces and moments. For physical locations:

> Put special items there to remind you that it's sacred:
>> your Bible
>> a photo of your children or pets
>> favorite stuffed animals
>> a stack of favorite Scriptures to read out loud[14]

- » essential oils or flowers that produce your favorite fragrance
- » a photo album (digital or physical) of your favorite memories and people (so you can say a prayer of thanks as you look through it)

> Use decorations to remind you that the space is sacred:
  - » walls covered with favorite colors, favorite quotes, and Scriptures
  - » plenty of pillows in your favorite colors and designs
  - » a poster board to write prayer requests on
  - » a sketchbook, coloring book, or canvas and whatever other materials you need to create your masterpieces

> Have materials and items in there that help you be creative:
  - » your favorite instrument so you can play a few chords or notes
  - » a journal for writing out everything you're learning and are thankful for
  - » pictures or pieces of art made for you by some of the children in your life
  - » a piece of art you created and saved from your childhood

Here are some sacred-space TinyHabits for any location:

> Sing a few lines of your favorite hymn.

> Close your eyes and take deep, slow breaths in through your nose and out through your mouth as you whisper a two-word prayer: *Thank You.*

> Breathe deeply and slowly for one or two minutes before and after work, perhaps while sitting in your car.

> Out loud, state three things you're thankful for.

> Take a two-minute meditation between each task in the day. (If you do this ten times a day, before or after ten tasks, you will become someone who is in the habit of meditating for twenty minutes a day.[15] It's a beautiful act of surrender—I like to use this time to work on the Bible verses I'm memorizing.)

I also suggest outdoor TinyHabits and locations (I've found that problems and sorrow often seem smaller when you can physically look up and around to see all that God can do and has already done):

> Go outside, smile, and turn your head toward the sun for a few minutes. If it's raining, stand in the rain for a few seconds and just smile.

> Pop up a tent on the back porch, zip it up, smile, and get lost in prayer and solitude for five to ten minutes.

> Sit in the grass, smile, and touch the ground for two minutes.

> Collect one small stone each day. Put the stones in a jar in your indoor sacred space to celebrate tiny steps toward healing.

> Smell or take a picture of a flower.

> Touch a tree, and thank God for our beautiful planet.

> Intentionally notice the sunrise, sunset, clouds, sun, moon, or stars each day.

As you practice these daily TinyHabits and create your own, you will incrementally become someone who is in the habit of inviting the sacred into daily life so you can receive and share the best gifts life has to offer.

Chapter 7

ARMOR UP AND TRAIN HARD

The Difference between Hurt and Harm

God doesn't want to use you. Abusive and manipulative
people use others. God wants to love you.

ABUSE, BETRAYAL, AND TRAUMA can distort and even destroy your ability to discover the calling God has for your life. And part of His calling is that He made you to love you. If you choose to accept His calling, as your relationship with Him grows, you will see how He will equip and empower you to be a part of His good work in this great universe.

In fact, we all have the same calling: "'Love the Lord your God with all your heart and with all your soul and with all your strength and with all your mind'; and, 'Love your neighbor as yourself.'"[1] The call is to love—that's all that's needed to revolutionize the world, one person at a time.

I vividly remember being nine years old and living in a homeless shelter. I can still feel the kindness of the volunteers who sometimes read us stories about Jesus, which I always enjoyed. But there was one time when the woman stopped reading, smiled at me, and asked, "Juni, do you know that God loves you and that your life is a gift from Him?"

I immediately responded, "Did God keep the receipt?"

As a trauma survivor, maybe you've heard the call and decided to go to church only to hear from the pulpit over and over again, "God loves you, and He wants to use you to accomplish His will."

Maybe, as I did, you sat there uncomfortably, wondering if you wanted to have anything to do with a god who makes people and then manipulates them into submission so he can use them. I remember thinking, *This god wants to use me? Tell him to take a number and get in line.*

What kind of parent *uses* their child? An abusive one. And trauma or not, every one of us interprets what we hear and experience through the lens of our worldview. Even as a teenager, I was able to see that healthy parents love in ways that encourage growth. They don't use their children to satisfy or meet their needs. They invite them into the adventure of life, help them learn their gifts, and inspire them to chart their own course. They enjoy them and love them for who they are—not for who they want them to be. And as these children learn and grow through healthy love, they create lives that honor their parents and make this world a better place.

Still, I couldn't ignore the call. I wanted to know God, so I kept on showing up, praying, studying, and asking questions. It didn't take long for me to realize that God is the perfect parent. The more I got to know Him, the more our relationship grew, and the more I understood what real love means.

If you have loving parents, no matter your age, you want to honor them. You want to spend time with them and share life. Your relationship is ever alive, growing, healthy, strong, and not codependent.

Unhealthy, abusive parents use their children to make them look good, fulfill their plans, and satisfy their desires.

God is the perfect parent. He doesn't want to use you—because He doesn't need anything. There is absolutely nothing that can interfere with His will and purpose for this world. He's a good Father who deeply loves and enjoys you for who you are. Every day, He continually invites you to accept His love and to participate in His good work, if you want to. And then He wants you to echo and overflow His love to the world in the unique way only you can. This choice is always available, because real love must always be a choice.

His daily invitation is for you to follow Him, learning, playing, growing, sharing, and serving out of the overflow of His love. This is the life that honors God and helps others know what He is like. As Jesus clearly said, this is eternal life: to know God and the One whom He sent.[2]

Real Love Does No Harm

"Love hurts sometimes. Everyone knows that," she tearfully said, as she continued to justify the ongoing emotional abuse she'd been excusing for decades.

I listened and then gently reminded her that I never said that love doesn't hurt. I said, "But love does no harm—there's a big difference."[3] This was a lesson I'd learned the hard way. It cost me in incomprehensible ways.

Most of us learn some idea of love through our earliest experiences in life. The messages—or lack of messages—that our primary caretakers teach us about their definitions of love stay with us for life—for better or for worse.

If it's for worse, we grow into the habit of seeking out and excusing abusive behavior in our relationships. This is true partly because no one wants to feel alone, but mostly because we're looking for what feels familiar. We're seeking out suffering that feels like home.[4]

But if someone is in the habit of hurting you—and they know they're hurting you—that's harmful abuse, not love. And it needs to stop. Being alone is always better than being abused.

Love builds up, strengthens, and encourages. Harm destroys and tears down. When you spend time with someone who loves you, you feel inspired and challenged to accept new ideas. You both walk away feeling accepted, safe, strong, challenged, and brave. You don't leave feeling beaten down, sad, ashamed, and wondering how to avoid the next encounter.

With real love, even conflict leads to growth and unity because you know you and the other person are on the same team, working toward shared aspirations.

Counterfeit love generates division and feeds on drama, negativity, strife, and confusion. It creates ever-disintegrating relationships because it's harmful. This false "love" wounds your body, heart, mind, and soul. Relationships that are characterized by it can emotionally cripple you.

The kind of people who habitually behave this way don't care if their decisions and words hurt you. No matter how you try to communicate about the hurt they're causing you, they keep doing exactly what they want to do to satisfy their needs and desires. They behave selfishly because it's easier and safer than learning how to love well.

These are the people who drain your energy and leave you feeling used up, devalued, and depleted. They only look out for themselves, and when you bring this to their attention, they justify their behaviors and often blame you. They don't say they're sorry, and—most revealing—they never change, even when they know they're causing harm.

They systematically block your access to peace and joy because they've never known it themselves and the longing for it frustrates and confuses them. If they're pretending to know God, they may use Scripture to demean, confuse, shame, and keep you under their control.

In the community of faith, a misunderstanding of the loving command to honor your father and mother has created generations of people who live every day exhausted, confused, wounded, and scarred because their parents are abusive and manipulative. If a spiritual leader in your life is encouraging you to move physically toward abusive parents, please don't listen. Always be kind and pray for your parents, but don't actively engage until you see sustained change for good. God is not a god of confusion.[5] He does not want you to be abused.

I live every day with a hard truth: My parents did not love me. But I forgive them because they simply didn't know how to love.

This truth hurts and has caused me great harm, but it has

nothing to do with my worth in this world. I know that because they chose not to do the necessary work to recover from their own childhood abuse, they never learned how to give or receive real love.

Telling children of abusers to excuse and enable abuse by continuing to move toward their unhealthy, unsafe parents is a disgrace. It's never honorable to willingly offer yourself up to absorb the damage and consequences of another person's evil and selfish decisions. Abusive parents are unloving parents, and you were not put on this planet to enable their abuse. *That is not God's plan for your life.*

The way to honor your mother and father if they are dishonorable is to create healthy boundaries. This means creating, practicing, and cultivating habits that will empower you to respond to them in ways that are healthier for both of you. They may not respect your boundaries at first, but you can carefully choose your responses to their disrespect so you don't get caught up in the drama all over again. Hold your head high, be brave, live out God's love, and shine bright. That's what honors God *and* your parents, no matter how unsafe and unhealthy they are.

It's also important for you to know that you don't owe your parents for your life. I mean, who could ever repay such a debt? You didn't ask to be here, but you can design and live your life in an honorable way that brings life, encourages growth, and makes this world a better place—one tiny choice at a time.

Never Abandoned, Never Alone

A few years ago, the headlines were filled with stories about an internationally known superstar pastor accused of multiple counts of sexual harassment. As the months passed, the accusations increased; finally, the worst one of all appeared in the *New York Times* on a Sunday morning. Eventually, the entire leadership team stepped down, and thousands of people all over the world were left devastated, confused, heartbroken, and hurting.

As I prayed for this pastor and my friends who were hurting because of his decisions, I remembered a sermon he shared in which he discussed his relationship with his father. He described how one time, when he was eleven years old, he told his family he wanted to learn how to ski. Soon after, his dad got him some skis, drove him to a bus stop, bought him a ticket, waved goodbye, and said, "Figure it out—don't call me."

And that's exactly what the pastor did. He was eleven years old, abandoned and unprotected, alone in a strange town. He said that this kind of thing happened repeatedly in his growing-up years.

Over and over again, he heard those words: "Figure it out— don't call me." I remember him ending this story with words of gratitude to his father for teaching him good lessons about independence, resourcefulness, and leadership.

I profoundly disagreed with the father's logic in placing an eleven-year-old in harm's way to teach him a lesson. I thanked God for protecting this pastor all those years while he figured it out on his own. I could see the good that came as a result of his resourcefulness, courage, and leadership. But there is no excuse for the mistakes this pastor made along the way to worldwide fame in the faith community. I wondered if the abusive decisions that made the international headlines—which directly harmed many and indirectly hurt several thousands of people who admired him—were, in part, fueled by unresolved, unprocessed pain.

I wondered how this harmful, so-called love from his father affected the pastor's view of God. It wouldn't be a stretch for him to secretly or subconsciously wonder, *If God is a "loving" Father, would He also drop me off unprotected and afraid and say, "Figure it out— don't call me"?* Maybe if he'd learned how to trust his allies, he might have welcomed the strong accountability partners needed in order to manage leadership, fame, and constant temptation. Perhaps with the right allies and God's faithful guidance, this pastor may one day come back and tell us some of what he's learned about the true love of God as our Father and how there's no mistake God can't redeem.

God never says, "Figure it out—don't call me." He says, "Are you tired? Worn out? Burned out on religion? Come to me. Get away with me and you'll recover your life. I'll show you how to take a real rest. Walk with me and work with me—watch how I do it. Learn the unforced rhythms of grace."[6]

No matter what anyone says, you're never too far gone for God to reach and heal. God is a parent who promises to never abandon you to figure things out on your own. He's always happy to see you, and when you ask for wisdom or help of any kind, He's delighted to generously give it and to be there for you. He even stays up all night, singing over you for your entire healing journey.[7]

Stronger and Braver

You may have noticed that the title of this chapter is "Armor Up and Train Hard." My recommendation for this step in the journey is to armor up, because in order to recover from your trauma, you'll need to be stronger and braver than you've ever been. If you want to transcend your sorrow and make it to joy, you must learn how to guard your heart. You must be armored and protected by truth about your worth, knowing that no matter what happens, God is with you. For that reason alone, it's going to be okay.

Some people are just not safe. They're toxic. No matter the reasons they behave this way, they don't mind taking out their anger and unresolved pain on you. Jesus would unapologetically say that they are under the influence of pure evil—in fact, of the one who accuses and lies in order to block your path and keep you from finding the joy of the Lord.[8]

I know it's uncomfortable, but I want you to know that it's okay to recognize that someone you love is abusive. It's actually a loving act that can lead to healing for both of you. Don't waste your time trying to tell them what you've realized—they aren't listening.

Just continue to take sure, tiny steps (such as reading this chapter), and always pray for them, but stop giving them the benefit of the doubt. In time, they will see that you're no longer allowing them to write any more chapters of their misery story on your back.

Your wellness is not something they see as benefiting them. They won't be happy with your self-care choices, and they will let you know they're upset. You'll be accused and attacked in some way, but you must stand your ground.

This is a step for which you will most likely need help and strong support in order to keep moving forward. When tempted to move back toward an abuser, that's the time to call on and assemble the allies you strategically identified in chapter 6. These are the people you'll need to help you as you create loving boundaries between you and the unhealthy people in your life who don't want you to be well. It's very much like having a sponsor to help with recovery from any unhealthy addiction.

Your allies will help you be prepared for this, stay encouraged, and sort through it all. Your weekly Celebrate Recovery or support group meeting will be a great place to spend time with allies, meet new friends who understand, and grow in in the arts of listening, community, and prayer.

As I mentioned in chapter 1, I began trauma therapy when I was four years old. Some of the greatest gifts I've received for ongoing recovery have been tools to help me stand up to the unhealthy, unloving people in my life and say, "Enough!"

Creating good boundaries in your life is a healthy way to "armor up" and guard your heart. But boundaries are not enough—you must also cultivate the habit of responding in healthy ways. You do not owe your abuser anything, and you can walk away. If you feel physically unsafe, get to a safe place. If the situation calls for it, I pray that you will press charges. No one has the right to physically harm you or a good excuse for doing so, and it's not your job to protect them from the real consequences of their decisions.

Leaving is usually the best decision for both of you, especially if only one of you is interested in taking steps to be well. You will never find peace, a sound mind, and joy if you continue to allow someone to abuse you. Nor will you find these if you choose to betray and abuse yourself by continuing in a toxic relationship.

If your abuser has died, you can refuse to allow them to continue to harm you by taking good, steady, tiny, systematic steps toward wellness. The best revenge is to be well and overcome what they did to you. You don't have to live out the rest of your story wounded, broken, and hurting. You can emerge even stronger and braver than you were before.

You can always choose faith, hope, and love to systematically create a good legacy of your own. But you're going to have to armor up in healthy ways, and you're going to have to train hard to unlearn the lies you've been taught about who you are and what you're worth.

Good Intentions, Terrible Results

Over the years, you've probably encountered well-meaning people with good intentions who tried to offer comfort by saying something like this:

> "Just think—if it weren't for [name of your abuser], and
> if [event, past or present] had not happened, then you
> would not be the wonderful, caring, faithful, and strong
> person you are today."

I appreciate good intentions, but any time something like this is shared with someone who is hurting, both people walk away knowing deep inside that they've missed the mark. Something is deeply, spiritually flawed with this way of thinking, and it's not as helpful as we would all like it to be.

These are words that were offered to me by well-meaning friends, coworkers, and relatives many times and through many trials. But not one of those times did they bring me any lasting comfort. Every time I heard them, I was appreciative of the love and concern they represented, but I secretly felt more confused, frustrated with God, and deeply sad.

Could it be that that the only way I could become the kind of person I most wanted to be was through the most heartbreaking experiences of my life? The parts I most desperately hoped to forget?

What you and I have been conditioned to accept is that we wouldn't be anything worthwhile were it not for the events, scenarios, and choices that have caused us the most pain. This flawed theory is meant to provide comfort and serve as an explanation for why bad things happen, but it actually reinforces the concept of owing someone for something. And if we owe so great a debt, how could we possibly hope to repay it?

The worst part of this idea is that you may start to believe that God's only way of revealing and strengthening the best parts of who you are is through the most horrible situations imaginable and the choices of people who are abusive, selfish, and cruel.

Though many of us try and try again, we stumble and get stuck in unhealthy relationships and situations with those to whom we think we owe so much—all because of a mistaken belief born of good intentions.

Please remember—write this on a sticky note if you need to— you don't owe an abuser anything. You don't owe them credit or appreciation. You owe them nothing.

The strength, creativity, courage, resourcefulness, compassion, and faith you have are gifts that God gave you. They are precious treasures that your abusers and their harmful actions couldn't touch. They are sacred parts of you that God has sheltered deep within you because they are part of His good design for you. You are His masterpiece.[9]

God doesn't need to use evil to equip us with virtue, character, and faith. If that were true, then heaven would just be an illusion. Remember: He doesn't *need* anything to accomplish His will. God is a master artist, and all the wonderful parts of your personality that you most value and are most appreciated by others are a beautiful, eternal pronouncement of His unique, loving, artistic expression through you. These good personal qualities were not meant to be revealed or created through abuse and trauma. Beethoven didn't need someone to beat the symphonies out of him. He just needed to practice, and that's exactly what he did.

If it's continually ignored, your unaddressed, unacknowledged trauma will create more sorrow in your life, which will overflow into this world. But no matter how many years have been swept up into the swarm of your pain, you can always move forward toward good—if you want to.

A common justification for the teaching about our gifts being revealed through trauma is that God allows evil so that He can later use us to "comfort those in any trouble with the comfort we ourselves receive from God" for His glory.[10] But this only works *if you survive the trauma.*

And that's a very real *if.* Suicide, especially suicide among young people in the United States, is not declining—it's actually on the rise. It doesn't make sense to blame God for allowing and orchestrating traumatic experiences just to accomplish good. He's already accomplished a whole multiverse of beauty and good without it.

The unhealthy God-wants-to-use-you idea can cause people who are sincerely trying to move forward in faith to feel stuck instead, weighed down with guilt and shame because they believe they've failed God by not managing to have enough faith to persuade Him to stop the pain.

People who are wounded and hurting don't need Scripture flung at them—they need to be listened to, heard, and loved.

God does not need to put you through trauma to give you opportunities to comfort others. You can always comfort and come alongside another human being, even if you haven't experienced trauma. You just need to sincerely care. Again, the call is simple: It's just love.

Fast Food and Fast Forgiveness

When you feel discouraged and hopeless, it's easy to give in to the temptation to believe that all is lost. This belief is why so many choose to self-medicate and look for shortcuts to recovery.

After hearing a sermon or seeking spiritual advice, you may even try to "please God" by unleashing what I call *fast forgiveness*.

Fast forgiveness is a lot like fast food because it doesn't work: With fast food, there's no deep nourishment or satisfaction, which is why it leaves you feeling hungry. Fast forgiveness is the same spiritually, emotionally, and mentally: Over time, it makes you and the person you're sincerely trying to forgive sicker and unhealthier.

In the internationally bestselling book *Boundaries*, the writers explain the following:

> Many people are too quick to trust someone in the name of forgiveness and not make sure that the other is producing "fruit in keeping with repentance" (Luke 3:8). To continue to open yourself up emotionally to an abusive or addicted person without seeing true change is foolish. Forgive, but guard your heart until you see sustained change.[11]

Creating boundaries is an act of love toward yourself and the person who's in the habit of harming and mistreating you. It's important to take it slow in matters of forgiveness. Because of the complexities of human relationships, forgiveness is not a one-and-done experience. It's more helpful to think of forgiveness as a process in which healthy growth is monitored along the way.

When you make the hard decision to get help and stay on your healing journey by creating boundaries between you and your abuser—whether that person is living or dead—any tiny step of progress you make is worthy of a Tiny Celebration.

I know it's difficult, but I believe you can do it! Your life is a direct result of what you believe you deserve. Every decision you make flows from this belief.

Though you can appreciate lessons learned from what you've

been through, it's unnecessary to force feelings of appreciation for it. I was often frustrated when I heard people say that they were thankful for the trauma they'd survived. I think it's helpful to admit that you would rather not have been through it.

I'm not thankful for my trauma. I'd love to have a different origin story. I'm not ashamed to say so, because truth invites healing. It's okay to acknowledge that you would have chosen an easier and less painful path for yourself.

To recognize what you've lost, to name what's been stolen from you, to face your true feelings about what happened—these are empowering first steps. They will help you begin writing new chapters in your story.

Don't fall into the fast-forgiveness trap. Instead, take wise and measured steps toward forgiveness. Always wait for sustained change. Gather advice from your counselor and allies if you get confused, but never rush back into dangerous relationships by sweeping harmful behaviors out of sight in the name of forgiveness.

Spiritual Martial Arts

What best describes you? Are you creative? Hospitable? Do you have lightning-fast wit? Are you a systematic problem solver and strategist? Are you determined and resolute? Are you able to stay calm under pressure?

Are you a compassionate, focused listener? An expert gardener? A gifted hairdresser? How about a reliable leader? Are you great with your hands? Do you pay incredible attention to detail? Are you skilled at learning languages? How about writing? Martial arts?

Long-distance running? Cooking or baking? Are you the silly, fun, nerdy one? The super creative designer? Are you a geeky, adventurous sci-fi nerd like me? Or the one with that great sense of humor who's delightfully goofy? Are you easily amused? Do you have a rock-solid faith that can't be shaken no matter how bad things seem?

I could go on and on, but I hope you see where I'm headed here—these are just a fraction of the hundreds of thousands of cool, quirky things that we can celebrate every day as we move forward, designing and using TinyHabits toward trauma recovery.

What are all the wonderfully fun, good, and unique things about you that you enjoy and love to share? You may have forgotten about them because of the drama, trauma, betrayals, and chaos. But they're still there, waiting to be uncovered, discovered, and enjoyed.

This section is designed to help you begin to discover these personal gifts and then grow them through careful, prayerful, and consistent use. As you accept and participate in your recovery using TinyHabits, you will begin to see more and more who you are apart from the situations that wounded you and created your sadness and sorrow. You will begin to discover what it means to live with peace and hope-filled purpose. Once you've achieved this state of being, your identity will shift incrementally from daily heartache to peace and then to joy. You will be able to overcome anything this often unkind world might bring your way.

Everything rises and falls on your degree of determination. This is the "train hard" component that's essential for you to master if you want to keep moving forward. You have to be willing to do the work.

For three years, I trained in Olympic-style boxing. My coach, Greg Young, always reminded me, "You can't think your way to victory in a fight." You have to train hard and practice so much that when the time comes in the ring with your opponent, it's all instinct. Greg also taught me that fighters have to "ignore the crowd and listen only for [your coach's] voice. That's how you'll win!"

I think of the TinyHabits specifically designed for soul-care as *spiritual martial arts*. With continual practice (just as in any martial art), you advance incrementally as you begin to see shifts in your strength as well as in your perspective about what you're capable of in every area of life.

The fact that you are reading this book means that you have been gifted with a measure of faith. Because God is the source of all that's good and because you're making progress in your self-care, it's clear to me that you already have the ability to follow God's prompting. You need only to learn how to listen to His voice.

It's not about failure to pray the right prayers or do all the right religious things. Any prayer—no matter how tiny—is the *right* prayer. Think about it: You're talking to the almighty God! That's exciting!

I've found that the most effective TinyHabit prayers are just a few words. For example, *Thank You, God* is a perfectly grand prayer! It's one of the most eloquent prayers you can pray, because strengthening the habit of appreciation and gratitude can change everything in your life. When you thank God for the gifts He's designed you with, it's an affirmation of love toward yourself and a simultaneous offering of appreciation toward Him.

So try it out. Try saying this out loud:

"Thank You, God, for my gift of _____. Help me use it today for good and for Your glory."

It's that simple. Thank God for the positive attribute that comes to mind, lather, rinse, and repeat.

You may feel a little weird, as if you're talking to yourself or as though your prayers are just "bouncing off the ceiling," as my best friend once said to me. If that happens, just remember that everyone talks to themselves all day long every day—it's called thinking! God hears you. Be patient—He answers every prayer.

Neuroscience has proven that your brain chemically processes and responds to tiny successes in the exact same way that it rewards you for big successes. So your inner reward is tiny, but it's essential toward victory over sorrow. You won't feel or see the results immediately, just as with any martial art. But with every celebration of gratitude, you're retraining and reprogramming your mind toward good, and incrementally detoxing it from the negative.

One of my favorite examples of what it means to train hard, one tiny choice after the next, is found in the 2010 remake of *The Karate Kid*. It's the story of a kid named Dre who is being constantly bullied. Every day his bullies seek him out to humiliate and harm him. One day he tries to strike back, and they chase him and beat him without mercy. Then suddenly a man named Mr. Han shows up and saves him.

Shortly after this, Mr. Han agrees to train Dre. Every day he teaches him a brand-new, tiny skill toward mastery. Some of them are so small and repetitive that they don't seem to make any sense at all. In time, Dre learns to trust his teacher, and with much hard work and practice, he wins a tournament and rises up strong and skilled in ways he had never dreamed he could.

Shortly before he wins the competition, Mr. Han explains how their journey together has proven that "life will knock us down, but we can choose to get back up."[12]

The trusting relationship that develops between Dre and Mr. Han during their training sessions is a perfect example of what it's going to take for you to live a victorious life despite your sorrow: making the right alliances and guarding your heart with wisdom, determination, training, and perseverance.

You must learn to trust your allies, and you must commit to showing up every day to do the repetitive work of learning how to care for your body, mind, soul, and spirit.

You must strengthen the habit of looking for, finding, and noticing what's good. And you must understand and practice the sacred, spiritual art of rest and surrender. Just like in *The Karate Kid*, every tiny, good step strengthens and prepares you for the next. Sometimes it will feel as if you're not making any progress, but I can assure you that every tiny time you succeed in choosing something that's healthy for you, you're incrementally growing and changing your story for good.

Over the years, I've heard many people say that they stopped praying because it didn't seem to make any difference. The truth is that every decision you make to sincerely turn your attention toward God is a good and effective tiny step toward joy. With every prayer, your identity shifts from being someone who gets lost in self-pity to someone who is in the habit of choosing faith.

If you decide to get out of bed in the morning, fix yourself a cup of coffee, and sit outside in the sunshine instead of lying in bed wracked with depression, celebrate that tiny victory every time.

As you persevere and cultivate the habit of celebrating every tiny step you take in your healing journey, you will find your joy and peace increasing. If you're still doubting and wondering about who you really are, and if you're having trouble separating yourself from your sorrow, I understand. I've been there.

The secret to breakthrough is right here: Think of a time when you were truly happy. You felt safe, full of hope, and overjoyed. You were fully present and enjoying the moment. Picture that scene, and know this: The person you are when you are feeling sincerely joyful? *That's the real you.*[13]

This is the outcome of true discipleship: to be with God in such a way that you fully realize who He created you to be. You are His beloved child and a citizen of the light[14]—you help others know what He is like.

My sister is a Celebrate Recovery leader, and she always reminds me that the healing journey is often two steps forward and three steps back. Please don't berate yourself for lost ground on any given

Tuesday. *Rest, recover, and reboot*, as I like to tell myself. Keep moving forward. "Always pray and never give up."[15]

By the way, you've done some really good, hard work today by reading and considering what I've shared in this chapter. Well done!

TinyHabit #7: Spiritual Martial Arts

Life is not about the destination—it's all about the journey. God is not interested in your accomplishments. He is interested and invested in the person that you become—the person He designed and created you to be.

This entire process of creating, testing, and practicing TinyHabits is a skill. And as with every other skill you have, you will need to practice regularly. Every tiny time you choose to proactively engage in this process, you grow and move one step closer toward who you were created to be.

Always keep it simple: Scale it down to make the desired behavior tiny—as tiny as you can. Then test and iterate, as we say in the start-up community. If it moves you toward your desired outcome or aspiration, do it again and again and again.

In time, your identity shift will occur, and you will become the kind of person who is in the habit of . . .

> choosing kindness
> being responsible
> choosing faith
> being dependable

> choosing prayer
> working hard
> studying Scripture
> showing up
> resting well
> being brave
> choosing hope
> listening well
> being present
> showing hospitality
> sharing hope
> offering encouragement
> sharing a smile
> reaching out
> looking up
> making peace
> finding the good
> organizing chaos
> noticing the details
> bringing help
> casting the vision
> rallying the team
> celebrating the good
> offering solutions
> making connections
> being prepared
> living out love

Think about the habits you currently have and what they're manifesting in your daily life. Are you seeing good results in your relationships? How about your physical and mental health? How about professional aspirations? Which habits are moving you toward your desired objectives, and which habits do you most want to create a Master Plan to get rid of?

Two things cannot occupy the same space at the same time. TinyHabits help you create habits and behaviors that will replace the behaviors that lead you toward undesirable outcomes. I always suggest starting with prayer.

I pray that you'll decide today to accept God's power to overcome your trauma by committing to armor up and train hard as you choose to walk by faith—for good and for life.

Chapter 8

FAITH AND VODKA

A Lifestyle of Tiny, Healing Choices

It ain't about how hard you hit. It's about how hard you can
get hit and keep moving forward—how much you can take and
keep moving forward. That's how winning is done!

ROCKY BALBOA

EVERY NIGHT: prayer, Bible reading, vodka, sleeping pills, anti-depressants, and then—she hoped—sleep. For years, this university professor, parent, and successful business owner ended each day with this exact routine. By all outside appearances, she had success in the game of life. She was credentialed and comfortable, yet she was restless because of sorrow directly caused by childhood trauma.

Her attitude about the good things in her life, including her faith and relationships, was strong and positive. Still, her overall health was incrementally declining. My friend and I would often talk about her bedtime habits and routine because I was extremely concerned about the dangerous combination of alcohol and prescription pills. But her explanation was always the same:

All I need is a whole lot of Jesus and just a little vodka. It helps me to know there's something I can do to numb the pain inside. It gives me the feeling that I have control over something in my life, and hope that I may get the rest I need. Plus, I'm not dead yet, so it must be working.

I'm not dead yet, so it must be working?

This statement from my friend speaks volumes about the unhealthy—even dangerous—choices we often make when we've run out of ideas for how to manage sadness and sorrow. In the moments when we're making split-second, autopilot decisions about how to numb and relieve pain, we don't realize that we're actually out of control. Those are the moments of self-deception when we're the most unloving and unkind toward ourselves.

This is why it's important to design your life in such a way that you'll never run out of ideas for your next tiny, healing choice.

Why Willpower Won't

One of the reasons I put my major-market morning-show radio career on hold to instead teach Behavior Design is because the concepts, models, and methods apply to all human behavior in every context.

During my seventeen years of hosting live radio, I received thousands of calls, emails, and messages from people who wanted to grow in faith, hope, and love, but no matter how hard they tried, they kept failing. Worst of all, they blamed themselves and worried that God was disappointed in them too.

It's exactly as Jesus says, on a global scale: "The spirit is willing, but the flesh is weak."[1]

I decided that I wanted to help people understand that it's not their fault and that God is not disappointed in them. He knows that most people simply don't understand how human behavior actually works. It's not a moral failing or a design flaw—it's a lack of understanding about how to design your life for daily victory. You only know what you know, and God is the perfect parent— He does not frown down at you for what you don't know about the healing process. Remember, God is a systems guy. He's orderly, not chaotic. Human behavior is systematic, so you simply need to understand the system. When you do, there are very few personal aspirations you can't succeed in for good.

The guidebook you're reading represents more than twenty-five years of prayer, research, and practice. TinyHabits create positive disruptions for good in every area of our lives. Change happens best when we feel good, which is how Tiny Celebrations reprogram our minds. Once you master this skill, you will never run out of good, simple, helpful ideas about what tiny, healthy choices to make next.

Now, to keep both of us moving forward, we need to spend some time talking about willpower.

When it comes to the shift in your mindset toward the healthy, good habits you want to create, it's helpful to imagine from now on that willpower doesn't exist. This understanding is the first step toward a better future.

Think about most New Year's resolutions and how those turn out. As you look back and try to figure out what went wrong, the shame, blame, and self-condemnation cycle begins. These negative feelings create an undercurrent of disappointment and exhaustion that robs you of motivation, and the resulting stress often interferes with getting the rest that you need. Perhaps the most frustrating part of all is the fact that when we get stuck in this cycle, we often begin behaving in ways that make the problem worse.

Before I understood Behavior Design, whenever I failed to stay away from cookie dough and bubblegum ice cream, I'd blame myself. Every day, I felt disappointed and defeated in this area. I believed that if I had more faith, I would find freedom from the addiction.

I was so wrong about this. And like billions of other people over the span of human history, I didn't know any better. I believed what my culture had taught me. I'd give up the goal until the next New Year's motivation wave hit. I would then start working out harder, while both the number on the scale and the sadness at the root of my problem remained the same.

We've all been there: wondering why we can't seem to do the things we most want to do. Hundreds of years ago, even the legendary apostle Paul (who wrote much of the New Testament) struggled with this deeply discouraging and frustrating willpower-based mindset in his journey of faith and healing. He wrote about it in a passage that reads more like a journal entry than an epistle:

> What I don't understand about myself is that I decide
> one way, but then I act another, doing things I absolutely
> despise. So if I can't be trusted to figure out what is best

for myself and then do it, it becomes obvious that God's command is necessary.

But I need something *more*! For if I know the law but still can't keep it, and if the power of sin within me keeps sabotaging my best intentions, I obviously need help! I realize that I don't have what it takes. I can will it, but I can't *do* it. I decide to do good, but I don't *really* do it; I decide not to do bad, but then I do it anyway. My decisions, such as they are, don't result in actions. Something has gone wrong deep within me and gets the better of me every time.

It happens so regularly that it's predictable.[2]

I'm so thankful for Paul's confession here. It's clear that any time you or I are feeling this way, God understands that we only know what we know. But if you are willing to learn how human behavior actually works and how to practice it toward mastery, you won't have to worry about falling into the willpower trap that Paul describes in his letter. With wisdom, strategy, and practice toward your desired outcomes—and God's help—you will succeed.

Equipped with the right tools and resolute practice, you can grow, heal, and accomplish aspirations you may think are out of reach. Willpower is unreliable and unsustainable because it was never intended to take us very far. God gave it to us to nudge us in the right direction. It's only and always a tiny, good prompt, like a notification on your phone. Even if it comes riding in on the "motivation wave," as we say in Behavior Design, it won't last. So if you want to keep moving forward, you need a system that always works.

If you read Paul's journal entry to completion, you'll see how he discovers the secret that sets us free from the guilt-shame-condemnation cycle created by putting our faith in willpower. He explains,

> The answer, thank God, is that Jesus Christ can and does [have all the power to help me]. He acted to set things right in this life of contradictions where I want to serve God with all my heart and mind, but am pulled by the influence of sin to do something totally different.[3]

This is not the Sunday-school answer, where you just say, "Jesus" and get a gold star. What Paul is revealing here is that when it comes to moving forward from trauma to faith, it's not about willpower—it's about God's will and His power.

God's will for you in recovery is for you to be well, empowered by His Spirit and equipped with the practical wisdom He freely provides each time you ask in faith.

Willpower surges and prompts you to make that next, tiny good move toward your objective. It also helps you pinpoint the things that really matter to you—the changes you know you need to make toward good. Willpower was never meant to sustain you, because that's God's job.

With each tiny, healthy choice you make, rooted in His love, you move one step closer to freedom, as you shift incrementally into the kind of person you were designed to become.

You Can Definitely Do This

Good parents celebrate when their children do their best based on their abilities. It'd be wrong and cruel to demand that babies start talking three days after they're born. It'd be ridiculous to expect that elementary-school children would know how to drive—they can't even reach the pedals!

We lovingly celebrate our children based on their abilities to take action toward accomplishing age-appropriate tasks. Please remember: God is the perfect parent. He knows what you're capable of right now, in this moment. But do *you* know what you're capable of right now, in this moment?

To sustain positive change, it's necessary to get into the habit of thinking tiny and celebrating Tiny Behaviors according to your ability. Ability fluctuates based on many factors, including environment and context. For example, I am a long-distance runner, but I can't run a half-marathon if I find myself battling the flu on race day.

Understanding ability and the transformative power of tiny is a key component toward successfully designing a lifestyle of healing choices. For example:

> Can you run a mile today? Maybe not. Can you stand up and take two steps? If so, go ahead, and then celebrate: *"Yes—I'm getting stronger!"*

> Can you recover from decades of sadness and trauma in one therapy session? No, you can't. Can you think of one good thing you're grateful for right now? Most likely. Then go ahead—choose gratitude for that one thing. Then celebrate: *"I'm thankful, and I'm moving forward!"*

> Can you memorize Psalm 119 this week? Not likely. Can you memorize the first two words? Probably. (Hint: It says, "You're blessed."[4]) So go ahead, and then celebrate: *"I'm memorizing Scripture!"*

Note the way these Tiny Behaviors can be accomplished regardless of motivation or willpower. They take seconds or minutes—not hours or twenty-one days. Then they are followed by the Tiny Celebrations that affirm the good, tiny choices and wire the new habits into your brain. It doesn't take a set number of days to acquire a new habit, because it's all about motivation, ability, and prompts. For example, a teenager doesn't need twenty-one days to acquire the habit of using a new phone! TinyHabits work the same way.

Regardless of your context or environment, you always have some level of ability to move toward your desired objective—and the tinier and more specific the behavior, the better. As long as you're consistent, the accumulated positive results are the same.

Based on your ability in any given moment, when you're prompted to act, take that one, specific, tiny, good step to move toward your objective—and then immediately celebrate. I believe with all my heart that God is celebrating that tiny step toward good right there with you! Any loving step toward good is a step toward Him, because He is the source of everything that's good.[5]

God knows it's the baby steps and the progress we make through practice that lead to identity shift and lasting change. And He knows better than anyone that this is very difficult, wildly courageous work. He's the master of tough love that does no harm. Sometimes He's more like Rocky Balboa than Mr. Rogers. He loves you too much to leave you the way you are. As Rocky famously said to his son, who was drowning in self-pity and making excuses:

> Let me tell you something you already know. The world ain't all sunshine and rainbows. It's a very mean and nasty place. And I don't care how tough you are—it will beat you to your knees and keep you there permanently if you let it. You, me, or nobody is gonna hit as hard as life. But it ain't about how hard you hit. It's about how hard you can get hit and keep moving forward—how much you can take and keep moving forward. That's how winning is done![6]

Clicking "Like" on Your Own Posts

As you practice your TinyHabits, don't worry if some of them don't work out the first time. This is a new skill, and if something isn't working, it might mean you need a new anchor or prompt, or maybe a new, simple Tiny Behavior. One of my favorite life rules is that you have not failed if you've learned something new and helpful.

Keep on testing and iterating your growth levers, as we say in the start-up community. You'll increasingly feel empowered and equipped to keep moving forward.

You know the teeny-tiny good feeling of affirmation you feel when someone "loves" your post on Instagram, "likes" your post on Facebook, or retweets your newest epiphany on Twitter? That tiny, good feeling happens because, as human beings, we need affirmation as much as we need air, food, and water. Now you know how to activate and maximize this gift without using one byte of cellular data. Your Tiny Celebrations produce the feeling of Shine, that tiny blast of dopamine (the feel-good hormone) that keeps you coming back for more.

The affirmation is caused by making the best choice for yourself to the best of your ability. In that instant, it's all that you need to keep moving forward. For most people, as confidence and ability increase, they inspire the next good and healthy choice. It's like clicking "like" on your own posts. Positive self-affirmation done right is a loving act of self-care.

I'm always encouraged when I think of the friend I mentioned earlier. She loves Jesus with all her heart and was doing many good things. In addition to working in her trade, she was going to church, memorizing Scripture, reading her Bible, praying, and even volunteering in her community. She was accomplishing lots of good for everyone else, but for many years, she couldn't find peace and sleep at night without prescription sleep aids and vodka. Overall, she was also someone I believed to be very good at self-care to manage depression.

But one day as we talked, I realized that something about her was missing. I said, "You have always been good at self-care, and you've taught me so much. But do you love yourself? If so, why do you risk your life every night with vodka and prescriptions?"

That day, she realized that self-care without self-love might be practical, but it's ineffective in addressing the core issues created by trauma. People who have been abused learn to devalue themselves. But the love of God is never about performance, achievement, or credentials. You deserve to live the abundant life He gladly gave His earthly life to make possible for you.

I'm so glad she not only listened but also *heard* me that day. As she began to lovingly celebrate every tiny victory—even on her lowest days—she incrementally moved away from that dangerous habit. She told me, "Juni, I had a rough night and woke up feeling awful. I almost stayed in bed all day today, but I got up and made it to my couch. I'm proud of myself!" I was proud of her too. We celebrated together through quick phone calls and tiny text messages.

Because she stopped condemning herself for being a human with limitations directly caused by her trauma, and because she practiced TinyHabits to grow in self-love, she discovered that she no longer needed the vodka. Her sleep has improved, her energy levels are increasing, and her joy is on the rise.

It's not about being a super saint or a superhero—it's about the ability you have right now to make the next loving decision toward recovery. It's about doing the tiny next right thing in your healing journey.

TinyHabit #8: The Tiny Grief Master Plan

One of the first things I did after learning Behavior Design was design a way out of my sorrow and the bad habits it was producing. The system I'm going to share with you right now is one I created for trauma recovery called *the Tiny Grief Master Plan*.

This Master Plan enables you to design hundreds of victorious, surprisingly joy-filled moments into each day. As I tested my theories about the relationship between TinyHabits and recovery, I made a surprising discovery: All the changes I most wanted to make for good were hindered at the root by my feelings of sorrow related to my childhood trauma and grief over my mother's life and death.

Discovery is vital. A friend of mine who is an attorney says that *discovery* is a legal term. It refers to gathering evidence to prove a case. If you don't discover the root of your sorrow, you will stay stuck. Behavior Design and TinyHabits reveal that we can use our feelings of sadness and grief as prompts and anchors for new, tiny, good responses.

Right now, there are certain activities and bad habits you choose directly because of your sorrow. Start by making a list of all the bad habits you'd like to get rid of. This will help you specifically recognize the unhealthy—even destructive—habits your negative emotions have created. Then pick the one you most want to replace. (Focus on only one habit at a time in the beginning. Then once TinyHabits are mastered, you can tackle getting rid of several simultaneously.)

One of the habits I wanted to replace was seeking and finding some serious sugar. Eighteen months and fourteen pounds later, looking in the mirror was a reminder of my pervasive sadness and lack of self-control.

When your trauma-related sadness arises, what concrete, specific behavior happens?

Just fill in the blank. Your sadness causes you to engage in the following immediate behavioral response:

_____

_____

_____

Don't condemn yourself. Remember—this is a no-condemnation zone. You only know what you know, and you're learning a brand-new way! Acknowledge and identify this unloving habit, and love and respect yourself enough to be honest about it.

The system I'm suggesting works because when you're in pain and looking for something quick and easy to divert yourself, you will take action. As I shared in chapter 5, the Fogg Behavior Model reveals that for every behavior, there must be a *motivator*, the *ability* to take action, and a *prompt*. When these three components occur simultaneously, the behavior will occur.

When you're sad, the motivator is your desire to stop or numb the pain. The sadness is the prompt, because it's the thing that says, "Do this now" to relieve or numb the pain.

What is the current behavior you immediately choose when prompted by sadness? Is it helping or hurting you? A good way to measure this is to ask yourself the following questions: *Is this a loving behavior that's helping me? Or is it harming me and the people in my life? Does it bring joy or more sorrow?*

If it's bringing harm and producing sorrow, then it needs to go. Your life depends on it! Replace the harmful behavior with something helpful and good. And you can—every single tiny time you're prompted.

Remember, the sadness prompt is not your enemy. There's nothing wrong with your mind. That feeling of sadness comes from your mind and emotions doing precisely what God designed them to do: *alert you that something deep within you needs your loving attention, care, and healing.*

Be *thankful* for the prompt. This is part of how you curate the habit of gratitude. Then use the power of your amazing ability to choose to carry out one tiny and specific behavior. Then immediately celebrate to affirm this good work that keeps you moving forward in your healing journey.

The prompt of your pain means you're still here—and that's wonderful! No matter how you feel, don't give up! You're alive, and that means there's still hope.

The next step in the Master Plan is to find out exactly which responses will be most effective in helping you achieve what you aspire to. These responses need to be as specific and tiny as possible. Make sure each behavior is what we call "concrete," meaning that you know *exactly* how to perform it. This is important because it's impossible to design for vague abstractions. In my Behavior Design workshops, I encourage participants to create at least five or ten specific behaviors that will move them toward their objectives. Using this method will enable you to create a constellation of good, loving, healing, tiny choices to make each time you're prompted by your sadness and sorrow.

To sustain positive change toward good, it's essential that you get in the habit of thinking tiny. By scaling desired behaviors down to their tiniest form, you can carry them out easily every time. So choose the one behavior that's *easiest* for you to do. You must be able to take action. The behavior must also be something you truly want to do, and it must be effective in moving you toward your objective. This is the *golden behavior*.

Now, every time you're prompted by sadness, take that one, tiny, specific action.

Here's one example from my personal *Sugar Addiction Master Plan*:

OBJECTIVE: BEAT MY SUGAR ADDICTION

Anchor Moment	Tiny Behavior	Celebration and Shine
Feeling of sadness (I am thankful that my mind and emotions are working properly to alert me to my need for loving attention and care.)	Grab a sugar-free snack (I always keep one with me.)	Smile and say, "I'm awesome, and I'm sugar free!"
Prompt and motivator	*Ability and behavior*	*Wires the habit into your mind*

When it's mapped out this way, you can see that it's a sequence of three quick Tiny Behaviors informed by the Fogg Behavior Model: B = MAP. This is why it's a Master Plan. It's the scientific Behavior Model combined with the method of TinyHabits.

Every time I was prompted by sadness and the motivation to relieve it, I immediately used my ability to choose a tiny, healthy behavior: I chose to enjoy a sugar-free snack, which I made sure to always carry with me. I then immediately celebrated: I smiled and said, *"I'm awesome, and I'm sugar free!"*

If I was at home when I was prompted, I would think or journal about something tiny but good about my mom—something that made me smile. For example, she loved Winnie the Pooh, and every time I see anything related to that "silly old bear," I smile as I remember.

TinyHabits have also helped me realize that no matter how unhealthy someone is, there's often something good to appreciate about his or her life. *No matter how tiny, it matters.* It's important that you learn how to celebrate every tiny victory in your own healing journey. You must learn how to affirm and encourage yourself. Every tiny time you succeed, celebrate in a tiny, healthy way. You are worth celebrating!

The Tiny Grief Master Plan enabled me to beat a sugar habit I'd struggled with for as long as I could remember that had ramped up to an addiction after my mother died. In fewer than sixty days, I beat my addiction and lost fifteen pounds. I've never gained it back. The system meant no more guilt, shame, condemnation, or failure—only success and progress. Because of my Tiny Celebrations all day long, *it felt good and was actually fun!*

One more thing: When you get stuck—and you will get stuck, because you're learning a new skill—remind yourself that you're in training. Your objective during this time is to keep moving forward in order to go, grow, and know that you're worthy of wellness. This is God's will for your good and for His glory.[7]

Resolve to never miss out on any opportunities to celebrate. And have as much fun and be as silly with your celebrations as you'd like. This might sound very strange to you—it did to me at first too. But I can promise you that it works.

When it comes to designing a life not controlled by grief and sorrow, you have to do some things that are different—things that may feel weird and uncomfortable. That takes courage. But you've got this—I know you can do it.

After losing his wife, Joy, to cancer when she was only forty-five, C. S. Lewis wrote, "No one ever told me that grief felt so like fear."[8] At the root of your sadness rest a great many fears, and I know you often wonder if you're going to make it through. It's often fear that masquerades as sorrow. I believe fear is at the root of every sin that moves us further and further away from God.

I pray that you will take courage today and design your own Tiny Grief Master Plan. Resources for mastering the art of TinyHabits toward victory in every area of life are available on my website (junifelix.com).

Trauma is bad code. TinyHabits enable you to reprogram your mind as you learn how to habitually affirm and love yourself *the way God does.* He endlessly affirms every good, tiny choice you make as you move toward His good plan for your life.

And trust me—God knows the power of tiny! From the atoms, molecules, and individual cells in your body to the skyful of stars, God reveals what's truly beautiful and what true power—His power—looks like and accomplishes. He longs for you to access and recognize this power so you can walk in freedom to live from the overflow of His love all day long.

This is where the war ends. When you partner with God by designing your new lifestyle of tiny, healing choices, you no longer rebel against Him because of your pain.

Your Tiny Grief Master Plan is a customized system that will shine light into your darkness right when you need it. It reminds you that you are not a slave to the feelings created by the abuse you've experienced. With God's help, you can choose simple Tiny Behaviors to take control of your responses to the prompts of your sorrow. You can take back your life—one TinyHabit at a time.

Chapter 9

IRREPRESSIBLE

Deep in Wonder and Full of Joy

I'm sure you've confessed every sin you can think of, haven't you?
You need to understand that it's not a sin to have a broken heart.
Stop confessing, slow down, and let God heal your heart.

PASTOR BOB MOELLER

HE LOOKED AS THOUGH HE'D STEPPED straight out of the Wild West—he wore an old, sun-bleached hat, jeans that were torn and ragged around the ankles, a denim jacket covered with dirt, and worn-out black boots. He watched me quietly for a few minutes, and then he came over to share his thoughts. He smiled and said, "You know, the ones up here are just like the ones at the bottom of the mountain. You didn't have to hike up this far—they're all the same."

"No, they're not," I replied. "I've been collecting rocks almost all my life, and every one of them is different. They each have their own story to tell."

He looked at me like I was crazy and walked away.

According to my Fitbit Alta, at this point in the journey, I'd hiked about four and a half miles up the mountain trail. I'd collected some of the most beautiful and interesting rocks I'd ever seen.

My backpack was getting heavy, which meant that it was inventory time. This is when I examine the rocks I've gathered, one by one, to see which ones to keep and which ones to leave behind. I knew I needed to make room and cut down on the weight of the pack so that I could keep following the path until I reached the waterfall just ahead. I always find the most beautiful rocks at waterfalls.

I've collected rocks since I was ten years old. My ever-growing-and-changing rock collection has always been one of my greatest treasures. After my strange conversation with Wild West man, I felt a bit sorry for him. How could he not know that every stone is unique, valuable, and beautiful in its own way? I'm especially fond of the geodes I've found (only two on my own after all these years). They're rare and sometimes hard to recognize: From the outside, they're not too impressive—they look a lot like regular rocks. But inside is a world of shimmering, sparkling beauty that only God can see until we open them up. To open a geode without damaging it, you must be very careful, gentle, and patient. But it's worth it when you finally get to see the beauty inside. Some geodes even sell for thousands of dollars.

I'm sharing this with you because on the morning I began writing this chapter, I woke up thinking about geodes.

In many ways, the work that you and I are doing to move forward from trauma to faith is very similar to what it takes to find and open a geode. You have to get uncomfortable, stay on the right path, be patient, and maintain a mindset open to possibilities.

It's the only way to find the great treasures hiding within something that looks quite ordinary on the outside and can easily be overlooked.

"I See You"

Yes, it's a line from *Avatar*. And *Titanic*. And I think it was also in *Blade Runner*.[1] "I see you" helped director James Cameron reign as "king of the world" at the box office for many years. After watching *Titanic* for the twenty thousandth time, I started wondering why it resonated so deeply with me and millions (or even billions) of viewers all over the world.

So, as we say in my house, what do you do when you don't know what to do? Research! Thankfully, I didn't have to look far. My colleagues at the Stanford University Behavior Design Lab have done extensive research into the top human aspirations. The results of many of these studies have revealed that right at the top of the list of the most important human needs is the need to be seen, affirmed, and understood.

You can easily see this need expressed if you spend time with children. When they create something, they immediately want to show you and find out what you think. They prepare to sail down the slide at the park, but often before they do, they call out, "Dad, look at me!" They reach the bottom and ask, "Did you see me? Did you see what I did?"

We never grow out of these types of behaviors, because the need to be seen and understood stays with us. It's a human need that causes us to wonder, and even worry,

> *Did I succeed?*
> *How did I do?*
> *Did I get it right?*
> *Am I doing okay?*
> *Am I worthy of your attention?*

Some have called this need to be seen, understood, and affirmed the greatest human need. And it makes a lot of sense. We were created for love by love, and we're to overflow this love in community.

In healthy families and fellowships, we gain the chance to have this most basic human need met as we play, pray, learn, and grow throughout our lives. But trauma causes too many survivors to isolate as a way to protect against further pain.

One of the biggest problems with a mindset of isolation is that it creates fear, which hardens our hearts. This shuts us off from God's good plan for our lives. As humans, we become like the people we spend the most time with. We adopt their ways of thinking, speaking, and responding because they are the ones with whom we feel most seen, understood, and accepted.

If you're cut off from others because of pain and fear, you become what I call a *self-referencing entity*. You're left with only your own ideas and interpretations of your experiences. You become accountable only to yourself.

You tell yourself that no one could possibly understand—and you believe it. When your only reference point is yourself, it's like being the only resident on your own planet. This lifestyle is what causes many to become the non-player characters I mentioned in chapter 3. You can't lovingly respond to and engage with others because you're trapped in your own mind and ideas.

But if you're willing to align yourself with God's design for community, the door to true freedom opens wide, revealing the path toward the abundant and joy-filled life He's had planned for you all along.[2]

The Promise of Joy

One of my favorite promises of God is found in the book of John. Jesus was talking with His closest friends and telling them about His gift of joy. He said, "I have told you this so that my joy may be in you and that your joy may be complete. My command is this: Love each other as I have loved you."[3]

It's clear to me that joy produced by faith is an identity feature: It's comprehensive, completing, and eternal. Joy is made real when we become aware of the limitless power, love, and presence of God.

Joy is more than a promise Jesus makes, and it isn't just a concept designed to distract you from the reality of the hardships you're facing. God isn't cruel or manipulative—He wouldn't promise you something you couldn't attain.

Scripture says that in God's presence is fullness of joy.[4] Thankfully, He is—in deed and in fact—ever present and all-powerful. God holds everything in place, and He's everywhere. But to experience the joy of His presence, you must be determined to create the habit of seeking and finding Him at work.[5]

One weekend after the sudden passing of his wife's father, my pastor shared that his father-in-law had been a man who knew how to find the good in every situation. He was someone who overflowed with love, praise, and appreciation in every area of life. As a medical doctor who never retired, he served at a hospital in one of the toughest neighborhoods in Chicago every week until the morning he woke up and enjoyed his last cup of coffee on this side of glory.

This unforgettable tribute to his father-in-law's life and legacy is a perfect example of what happens when your greatest aspiration becomes seeking, finding, and celebrating God's goodness toward you. As you get to know God, your faith begins to grow—and as it does, it overrules your fears. In time, your gifts come alive, and genuine love, courage, and compassion become your most celebrated attributes.

If you are committed to growing in faith in order to know God and become more like Him, you gain the gift of His presence. You find rest and joy in His continual Shine, and the more you know Him, the more you love.

Jesus proved by His sacrifice that no one sees, loves, and accepts you more than God. In this life of faith, His gift is Himself. What parent would require that someone else go out to search for their lost child instead of going themselves? God didn't hire some messenger or send an angel to rescue you—He came Himself, in the person of Jesus Christ.

By faith, you accept the gift of His sacrificial love and receive His Spirit. This is how He enables you to walk in the truth. Through this, you can have as much of God's love and attention as you want as you travel together in the healing journey. As you experience the mysterious and healing love of God, He empowers you to stop seeing everything in your life through the lens of your pain. This is how you finally stop running, slow down, and gain the chance to break free from your trauma and begin finding your way home.

As you design your TinyHabits and continually fill your days with Tiny Celebrations and Shine, people will begin to watch and wonder about the source of your joy.

As you grow in your awareness of God's presence and in your ability to appreciate what's worthy of praise, you'll eventually find that you've overcome the world and are finally walking in and living out love. Everywhere you turn, you'll see reasons to give God praise, be thankful, and be fully present. You'll find yourself delighted by the simplest things, such as the bright red hat the lady in the bookstore always wears. You'll offer a thankful smile every morning with that first sip of good coffee or tea. You'll delight in the sunrise and the gift of the new day as you take a moment to be amazed and appreciative of the miraculous power that holds our sun in the sky.

The Third Heaven
I believe this is the kind of mysterious awareness the apostle Paul described in the second letter he wrote to the Corinthian church:

> I know a man in Christ who fourteen years ago was
> caught up to the third heaven. Whether it was in the
> body or out of the body I do not know—God knows.

He went on to explain that this man was "caught up to paradise" and learned "inexpressible things."[6]

I can't think of a better way to describe a life rooted in true joy. This is a life where each day you are the watchperson. You're on duty every waking hour, like a chief detective assigned to find evidence of God's goodness in everyday life. Then, when you find the proof, not only do you recognize it—you celebrate!

No matter how tiny the celebration, even if it's only between you and God in the secret place of your heart, you're the one who chooses to acknowledge what's good and praiseworthy.

This doesn't mean you ignore the reality of your situation or trivialize the pain and sadness in the journey. There are few things as unhealthy and damaging as unbridled optimism leading to denial and a tyranny of positivity. But it does mean that when dark times come—as they always do—you'll be a person who is equipped, ready, and willing to offer hope and shine the light. Even if you are the only one not panicking, your calming presence might remind others that no matter how much it seems that all hope is lost, it's somehow going to be okay.

My friend Donovan works six days a week as a spiritual first responder to families directly affected by the ongoing violence in the city of Chicago. He's helped hundreds of families take practical next steps toward renewal of hope after the murders of their loved ones. He is living proof that even if a moment is so horrible that it seems impossible to find the good hidden deep inside the sorrow, God's Spirit will serve as a reminder that you're never alone. God is with you in the tragedy and will strengthen you to make it through the pain.

A Lesson from Hulu

My sister Teruko frequently visits during the holidays. Whenever she stays with us, it's quite clear that she and I have very different tastes when it comes to entertainment. For example, I feel that I've had enough sadness, sorrow, and dark drama for a lifetime, so I prefer entertainment that's light and hopeful throughout—you know, Marvel superhero stories, clean comedies, and adventures overflowing with more wonder than woe.

She, on the other hand, has always preferred a good Tim Burton–style dystopian drama. During one visit, she insisted that I spend some time watching one of her favorite shows: a wildly popular, highly awarded Hulu Originals drama called *The Handmaid's Tale*.

I didn't make it thirty minutes into the show before I felt frustrated, deeply saddened, and repulsed by the relentless grey skies, ongoing peril, and terrible injustice I was witnessing scene after scene. Still, there was one line in the series that caught my attention. It captured my heart and helped me instantly understand why the show is so popular and why my sister wanted me to watch it with her. Near the end of the first episode, the main character proclaims, "I intend to survive. . . . My name is June."[7]

This caused me to cheer! I brightened up and said, "That's what I'm talking about!"

I share this with you now, as we're nearing the end of our time together in this chapter of your healing journey, for one specific reason: Your life will continue to unfold according to what you believe.

Words—both spoken and unspoken—have power, and if you believe you will overcome any darkness this all-too-often cruel and isolating world brings your way, you will do that very thing: You will overcome.

One of my favorite Scriptures is found in the third chapter of the book of Revelation. There, Jesus says,

> Behold, I stand at the door and knock. If anyone hears
> my voice and opens the door, I will come in to him and
> eat with him, and he with me. The one who conquers,
> I will grant him to sit with me on my throne, as I also
> conquered and sat down with my Father on his throne.[8]

Jesus' dream for us is not that we become experts at bribing or bargaining with God so we can get the things we want or the things we believe we most need. He didn't create us for some useless, frustrating game of "Who can be the most religious?" and "Who's the most successful, favorite child of God?" God is love, and He created you and me to show others what He's like.

In fact, the purpose of our lives is to love Him and show others what He's like. Blessings as they are commonly understood (health, wealth, worldly prosperity) only create in us the habit of coming to God to try to get more stuff. No one wants to be in a what's-in-it-for-me relationship, because that's not love. And it's not faith either.

The war ends when we realize that God is the blessing and the reward.[9] When we seek Him instead of ourselves, He blesses us with the knowledge of who He designed us to be, and He teaches us how to love well. He knows that we can only appreciate blessings when we fully understand and acknowledge that He is the source—and He never runs out of Himself.

The National Anthem in the Land of Joy

When you arrive at the destination of abundant life—"abiding" in God, as Jesus described it[10]—you'll understand the "inexpressible things." You'll finally be able to leave all the baggage behind as you take up residence in the land of His joy.

It's a forever place, where you are perpetually curious, delighted, amused, and appreciative. You are God's creation. He wants you to come home to Him by faith. With every tiny speck of good He can convince you to notice, you move closer to Him.

This is what it means to walk by faith and to know and be set free by truth. It's also my deepest prayer for you.[11]

At the beginning of this chapter, I shared something that one of my favorite Chicago pastors told me. He said, "Juni, I'm sure you've confessed every sin you can think of, haven't you? *You need to understand that it's not a sin to have a broken heart.* Stop confessing, slow down, and let God heal your heart."

The words above were spoken to me when I was drowning in sorrow but there was no time for sadness in my life. I was hosting my radio show, leading in several ministries, taking care of my two boys, and trying to keep my head above water.

The guilt I felt about my sorrow was like a millstone at the bottom of an ocean of sadness, tied securely to my foot. I swam with all my strength every day, but the millstone kept me from moving forward.

The pastor's words of truth cut the rope. Suddenly, I was able to swim to the shore. Without his help, I'd still be living a completely depleted, exhausted life, weighed down by sorrow.

He also taught me that sorrow is a gift. It's an invitation to take courage, slow down, rest, and grieve your losses—to switch to slow motion so you can hear the message that your sadness is trying to communicate so that you can move forward.

One of my favorite movies as a girl was Disney's 1993 retelling of the classic story *Heidi*, starring Noley Thornton. In the film, she has a bedside conversation with a blind woman she lovingly calls "Grandmother." As the woman is near death, she holds Heidi close and asks for a very specific promise. She says,

> You have a gift, Heidi—a way of touching the people around you, of helping them and bringing joy. But it can also be a curse, too, because it can use you up until there's nothing left—nothing left for yourself. So promise me, no matter how hard, that you will look deep inside and find out who you are. Hold onto it, Heidi, no matter what.[12]

This scene of loss carries a great message for you and me as we work hard to survive our sad seasons in this often cruel and isolating world. Sadness can consume you until there's nothing left. It can mute and even destroy the gifts you were born with so you can be a source of light and good in this world. In order to make it to the other side of your sorrow, you must decide to look deep inside and find out who you are *apart* from the situations and circumstances that have left you wounded and brokenhearted.

Whatever you're feeling right now won't last forever. No matter what you've lost or survived, there's a message in your sadness that can lead you to a place of peace and even joy. If you're wondering what it's like in this place, just listen to the lyrics to Pharrell Williams's 2013 hit song "Happy." It's just like that. It's the national anthem of the land of joy. You're meant to dwell in that land, where joy allows you to transcend anything this mean world throws your way.

Again, this is not an easy path. It is slow and, at times, arduous. Recovery is sometimes two steps forward and three steps back. Go ahead and fill to the brim that TinyHabits tool kit—fill it with strategies, systems, methods, and models that work for success and Shine. And please don't ever give up!

Always remember, you absolutely can't do this alone—and you were never meant to. Please seek out the safe people in your life and share your story. Ask them for guidance and support in finding the help you need—the help you deserve.

Your situation is not your destiny. Take courage, slow down, armor up, train hard. Learn your gifts and trust your allies. Love well, and do the work. Because you are so loved.

TinyHabit #9: A Lifestyle of Celebration

When it comes to what we give our attention to, you and I always have a choice. Ideas are powerful, and how we entertain ourselves—what we receive into our lives and allow to become part of our stories—is a critical factor in some of our most influential ideas. Yes, it's that deep.

The moments of your life are irreplaceable, and what you notice and give your attention to always costs something. Nothing is free in our linear, timeline-dependent lives. Every investment has a return. That's why we call it *paying* attention. So why not pay attention to the things that bring life, spark hope, and produce lasting joy?

You've already begun to practice the skills necessary to launch a lifestyle of celebration. Now, to take it to the next level, you must decide to *strengthen* the habit of seeking, noticing, and discovering praiseworthy things.

This is the most powerful TinyHabit of all because there's something supernatural and transcendent about gratitude and appreciation. This is the way God designed us, and it's how our desire for entertainment works for our good. Appreciation opens a portal to abundant life and brings healing to our souls and spirits. It sows seeds of joy every tiny time we choose it.

And it's simple—which is why it works! At every opportunity, you're doing something that many trauma survivors are experts in: finding and focusing on a specific set of thoughts. Only now you're doing it in reverse: Instead of focusing on what's wrong, you're focusing on what's good. It's important to understand that what you don't appreciate, you ignore, misuse, or destroy—but what you *do* appreciate brings new life. Gratitude transforms the ordinary into the extraordinary!

For this TinyHabit, you know what you need to do. But below are a few examples to get you started.

Anchor Moment: After I start the morning coffee,
Tiny Behavior: I will say, "Thank You, God, for whoever discovered coffee!"
Celebration and Shine: Then I will smile and say, "It's good!"

Anchor Moment: After I brush my teeth,
Tiny Behavior: I will say, "Thank You, God, for my teeth!" (or "tooth," depending on the quantity).
Celebration and Shine: Then I will smile and say, "Praise You, Jesus!"

Anchor Moment: After I see one of my loved ones,
Tiny Behavior: I will say, "I'm happy to see you!"
Celebration and Shine: Then I will smile and say, "I love you!"

Anchor Moment: After I finish a book to help me move forward from trauma to faith,
Tiny Behavior: I will snap the book shut!
Celebration and Shine: Then I will say, "Hallelujah! Onward!"

See—it's fun and easy! And humans love easy!

Noticing what's good and worthy of praise and appreciation requires creativity and genuine love. With practice, it becomes and remains the most valuable TinyHabit of all. And you don't have to take my word for it. God says,

> Don't fret or worry. Instead of worrying, pray. Let petitions and praises shape your worries into prayers, letting God know your concerns. Before you know it, a sense of God's wholeness, everything coming together for good, will come and settle you down. It's wonderful what happens when Christ displaces worry at the center of your life.
>
> Summing it all up, friends, I'd say you'll do best by filling your minds and meditating on things true, noble, reputable, authentic, compelling, gracious—the best, not the worst; the beautiful, not the ugly; things to praise, not things to curse. Put into practice what you learned from me, what you heard and saw and realized. Do that, and God, who makes everything work together, will work you into his most excellent harmonies.[13]

Every decision you make about what you will seek out, discover, and celebrate is like a keystroke in a line of code. You are programming your mind, influencing others, and designing your legacy.

Living a lifestyle of celebration inevitably transforms you into a joy billionaire—someone who sparks hope, encourages peace, and through kindness offers others a glimpse of what God is like. Choosing to celebrate what's good, no matter how tiny, snaps you into the present moment. It marks a mindful existence that invites us to rest in the reality that God is with us.

Celebrate the fact that the trauma you've experienced did not end your story.

Celebrate the strength God has placed deep within you that no abuse could take from you.

Celebrate that you are a survivor. More than that, you are more than a conqueror because of God's love for you.[14]

Celebrate the realization that even when you were young you were mightier than most because you persevered through the unthinkable.

You are clever, brave, and strong—like Wolverine in the X-Men. You've got healing power and the strongest element in the multiverse fused into your bones.

You're unstoppable, and your story is getting really good—one TinyHabit at a time.

Acknowledgments

Jesus: My Savior, my life—your glory, forever. No matter what.

Kai: Ours is a story of grace, prayer, and daily miracles. For me, computer programming was a gateway to another world; for you, a place to see the little girl who laughed at all your jokes. We made a mess, but it's our mess. I love your courage to believe the truth, break the chains, and shine God's healing light with me to end generations of broken promises and tragic endings. You will always be the Titus to my Yuna and the Bruce to my Natasha. Thank you for helping me win all the boss fights and find the hidden potions and remedies when my HP runs out, and for your ongoing encouragement and prayers. I love you.

Raphael: Fellow Inkling—your faith, compassion, and wisdom inspire me to be the very best I can be every day. It's an honor to grow with you and share the journey. I am overjoyed that God picked me to be your mom. Thank you for the endless laughs and deeply inspiring late-night and early-morning conversations.

Elijah Leonardo: "Lil Prophet" 😄 When you joined the team, we became the Fantastic Felix Four. I suddenly had two Ninja

Turtles, and we never looked back! Kiddo—you are a marvel and you can fly! Your mind is magnificent, and I'm constantly amazed by your courage, strength, creative energy, and joy! When I see you, I'm reminded that with God, all things are possible.

To my six beloved sibs:

We fuss, we fight, we get in each other's way.
We laugh, we learn, we make up games to play.
And when life takes its best shot, we unite to win this game.
No one loves me like my siblings,
when I'm weak, you share your strength.
(And this ain't no library!)

Auntie Diann and Uncle Billy: Thank you for everything—the prayers, the wisdom, the love, and the encouragement . . . always!

Dr. B. J. Fogg: Thank you for dedicating your life's work to discovering what I believe to be an $E = mc^2$-equivalent theory of human behavior. Your loving work is a gift of wisdom equipping me and countless others worldwide with tools that work toward personal breakthrough for good in exponential ways. You are one of the most caring, mindful, innovative, and brilliant teachers I've ever met. Thank you!

Stan Lee and Dallas Willard: From a fellow mutant-mystic-misfit—I'm grateful.

Marilyn: I can't believe you *still* have the letters! Whenever I think of running for public office (again), I remember the evidence and switch to Plan B. You inspired me to keep on writing before I ever knew that this would be a chapter in my story! To know you is to love you, and I'm so glad I know you best!

Debbie, Lena, and Rhiannon: Debbie, you taught me how to use my mind to break sticks in the woods as we imagined surviving the *Titanic* together. You were the first person to tell me that *lo que es para ti, nadie te lo quita*. Lenabear, your faith inspires me every time I think of you. Rhiannon, you're so loved.

Jennifer Epperson: You're always right on time, reminding me to suit up and boldly go where no man—or woman 😊—has ever gone before. I just love you!

Hannah, Cherise, Tinakka, and my Noo Noo Susan: My Chicago sisters! Hannah, thanks for teaching me how to find my style and how a little glitter is always a good idea. Cherise and Tinakka, without your prayers and encouragement, this book would never have happened. Susan, we're calamity cousins, journey mates, and prayer sisters forever!

Robin: Thank you for miraculously seeing pages of my story that were yet to be written. I'll always be grateful for the way that you opened your home to my family when we were teetering on the edge of sanity and hope. I'm looking forward to that green soup!

Don Pape: Are you gonna eat that? Thank you for listening when a "little bird" told you to reach out and for finding the typos on my website! You're a beacon of light, love, inspiration, and joy! Thank you for believing in me and flying to Chicago to buy me chili at Chili's and for asking, "So, are you writing anything?"

David Z.: On the day you were born, God said, "That's him!

My baby girl's editor!" On the day I was born, God said, "Give David some extra grace for later."

My team at NavPress and Tyndale House—Olivia Eldredge, Amanda Woods and Madeline Daniels, and Ron Kaufmann: Ron (and Robin!), you were Ethernet-wired to God's heart with this design! Thank you!!!

Judy Dunagan: Thank you for sharing your father's prayers with me long before we met in person. Because of you, this manuscript was written long before it had a home. You always remind me that though there are always unseen battles, God is greater, and he can do anything but fail. Your friendship means more to me than I could ever express. Thank you for coming alongside me in ways that very few could.

Stephanie Warner: My Time Lord and realm-building sister! Thank you for believing me when I shared "impossible" things from my years in Wonderland. For listening, praying, and helping me process the chaos and find hope when I was at the edge of my sanity. Please hug your papa for me. Your family is a blessing!

Don Hawkins, "Boss": So glad I have forever to thank you every time I see you!

Miriam and Aggie: Thank you for your ongoing prayers and encouragement to stay the course. Miriam, you read my first manuscript a million years ago and called it "excellent." When things got rough, you helped me stop "banging my head on the concrete ceiling" and follow God's lead. Aggie, thank you for reminding me to never hide my voice.

Compass Prayer sisters in faith: You know we got this! I love you ladies *so* much!

Team Puerto Rico and Kevin and Rebecca: I did it—I made all the deadlines! Thanks for your prayers! Sherri and Paul, thanks for letting me borrow your car!

Notes

INTRODUCTION
1. Kate DiCamillo, *The Tale of Despereaux: Being the Story of a Mouse, a Princess, Some Soup, and a Spool of Thread* (Cambridge, MA: Candlewick Press, 2003), 221.

CHAPTER 1: YOU ARE WORTH DOING THE WORK
1. See John 14:8-9.
2. Psalm 51:5, ESV.
3. Sharon Hersh, *Belonging: Finding the Way Back to One Another* (Colorado Springs: NavPress, 2020), 2.
4. This insight came to me from Pastor Bob Moeller, founder of For Better For Worse For Keeps Ministries.
5. Isaiah 53:3, NLT.
6. See Isaiah 61:1.
7. Mr. Krabs's first dime is featured in "Can You Spare a Dime?," season 3, episode 47b of *SpongeBob SquarePants* (aired on March 8, 2002).
8. Watch Dr. B. J. Fogg, the founder of Behavior Design and persuasive technology, explain the Maui Habit at TEDxMaui: https://www.youtube.com/watch?v=2L1R7OtJhWs.

CHAPTER 2: STRINGS AND MACROS
1. *Avengers: Age of Ultron* (Burbank, CA: Buena Vista Home Entertainment, 2015).
2. *Fight, flight,* and *freeze* only scratch the surface of how we may react when we face fears of the unknown. It's beyond the scope of the book to discuss

these at length, but some lesser-known responses include *please and appease* and *collapse and submit*. One of my favorite recent studies on this topic was completed by Stanford University in the summer of 2017. The experiment involved using a virtual reality simulation involving a great white shark. The goal was to "help people gain more control over irrational fear, a response that can get tripped off so often or so severely it hampers healthy coping." See Bruce Goldman, "The Fearful Eye: Using Virtual Reality to Hack Fright," *Stanford Medicine*, Summer 2017, https://stanmed.stanford.edu /2017summer/huberman-virtual-reality-curing-fear-anxiety.html for more on instinctual reactions to fear.

3. Proverbs 31:8, CEB.

4. Contact your local church for a list of PTSD-trained trauma-recovery specialists in your area. Celebrate Recovery groups are wonderful places to grow in faith and meet others who can make recommendations for trauma-recovery care: https://www.celebraterecovery.com/crgroups. You can also search here: https://www.psychologytoday.com/us/therapists /trauma-and-ptsd.

5. John 5:6-9, NLT.

6. *Toy Story 4* (Burbank, CA: Disney-Pixar, 2019).

7. See Proverbs 18:21 and James 4:2-3.

CHAPTER 3: THE CURSE THAT'S A GIFT

1. *The Matrix* (Los Angeles, CA: Warner Bros., 1999).

2. *Star Wars: Episode II—Attack of the Clones* (San Rafael, CA: Lucasfilm, 2002).

3. Luke 4:18.

4. "Celebrate Recovery is a Christ-centered, 12 step recovery program for anyone struggling with hurt, pain or addiction of any kind. Celebrate Recovery is a safe place to find community and freedom from the issues that are controlling our life." https://www.celebraterecovery.com.

5. See John 10:10.

6. Deuteronomy 11:26, MSG.

7. I can't remember which interview or event it was where I first heard Dallas Willard speak about this. But he is someone I consider to be a spiritual mentor, and even after his death his work continues to inspire and fuel my growth. Learn more about him and read some of his writings at https:// dwillard.org.

8. Nadine Burke Harris, "How Childhood Trauma Affects Health across a Lifetime," TED: Ideas Worth Spreading, September 2014, https://www.ted .com/talks/nadine_burke_harris_how_childhood_trauma_affects_health _across_a_lifetime/transcript?language=en.

9. See Matthew 5:16.

10. Philippians 4:8-9, MSG.

CHAPTER 4: THE JOY SET BEFORE YOU

1. See Galatians 5:22-23.

2. See Mark 4:14-20.

3. See Jeremiah 4:3-4.

4. Personal interview with the author.

5. Matthew 5:14.

6. 1 Thessalonians 5:5.

7. John 16:33.

8. *X-Men: Days of Future Past* (Los Angeles, CA: 20th Century Studios Home Entertainment, 2014).

9. Isaiah 53:3, ESV.

10. Hebrews 12:2.

CHAPTER 5: TAKE COURAGE AND SLOW DOWN

1. B. J. Fogg, *Tiny Habits: The Small Changes that Change Everything* (Boston: Houghton Mifflin Harcourt, 2020), 200.

2. Hebrews 13:15.

3. Philippians 4:8.

4. Please don't try to do this on your own. I have been in trauma recovery with the help of a professional trauma specialist throughout most of my life. When dealing with addiction of any kind, it's best to seek out the guidance of a professional trauma therapist. Most trauma specialists operate on a sliding-scale payment system based on income. Remember, you are worth doing the work, you do have time, you can afford it, and you can do this!

    The physiological effects of childhood abuse and neglect have been extensively researched, studied, and proven. Survivors are vulnerable to post-traumatic stress symptoms because during our formative years our minds and bodies have learned that we're perpetually unsafe. This produces elevated anxiety levels, fear responses, flashbacks, and disruptive memories that affect every physiological function. PTSD breathing techniques have been proven to help lessen these responses. Some of the most helpful studies on this topic include the following:

> Stanford Medicine's neurological study on how slow breathing induces tranquility: https://med.stanford.edu/news/all-news/2017/03/study-discovers-how-slow-breathing-induces-tranquility.html.

> Harvard University's study on how the persistent absence of responsive care disrupts the developing brain: https://developingchild.harvard.edu/resources/the-science-of-neglect-the-persistent-absence-of-responsive-care-disrupts-the-developing-brain.

5. Harvard University's study on Adverse Childhood Experiences (ACEs): https://developingchild.harvard.edu/resources/aces-and-toxic-stress-frequently-asked-questions.
6. See Psalm 139.
7. See 1 John 4.
8. See John 4:4-14.
9. The University of Tennessee–Knoxville and Texas A&M University did a compilation study of nearly fifty years of data from 138 studies involving more than eleven thousand participants globally. They concluded that the physical act of smiling influences feelings of happiness. Similar results were shown related to all physical-emotional activities and their influences on our conscious experience of emotions. See Nicholas Coles and David March et al., "A Multi-Lab Test of the Facial Feedback Hypothesis by the Many Smiles Collaboration," *PsyArXiv* (February 2019), doi: 10.31234/osf.io/cvpuw.

CHAPTER 6: LEARN YOUR GIFTS AND TRUST YOUR ALLIES
1. Fogg, *Tiny Habits*.
2. Individuals with certain cognitive disabilities will struggle with quickly responding or reacting.
3. See Matthew 12:43-45 and Luke 11:24-26.
4. See John 8:12.
5. See, for example, Psalm 147:3.
6. Romans 8:29.

7. If you're interested in becoming a master TinyHabiteer, check out https://tinyhabits.com.

8. Proverbs 18:1, NKJV.

9. "When People Show You Who They Are, Believe Them," *Oprah's Lifeclass*, OWN, aired on October 26, 2011: http://www.oprah.com/oprahs-lifeclass/when-people-show-you-who-they-are-believe-them-video.

10. Matthew 7:15-16, ESV.

11. Genesis 32:22-32, NLT.

12. Jim Wilder, *Renovated: God, Dallas Willard & the Church That Transforms* (Colorado Springs: NavPress, 2020), 48.

13. John 8:32.

14. For a list of some of my favorite encouraging Scriptures to read out loud and keep in your sacred space, visit https://www.junifelix.com.

15. Becoming someone who is "in the habit of . . ." is evidence of a true identity shift. This is one of the key incremental progress markers in Behavior Design.

CHAPTER 7: ARMOR UP AND TRAIN HARD

1. Luke 10:27.

2. See John 17:3.

3. See Romans 13:10.

4. See Alain de Botton, *The Course of Love* (New York: Simon & Schuster, 2016).

5. See 1 Corinthians 14:33, ESV.

6. Matthew 11:28-29, MSG.

7. See James 1:5 and Zephaniah 3:17.

8. See John 8:44.

9. See Ephesians 2:10.

10. 2 Corinthians 1:3-4.

11. Dr. Henry Cloud and Dr. John Townsend, *Boundaries: When to Say Yes, When to Say No to Take Control of Your Life* (Grand Rapids, MI: Zondervan, 1992), 36–39.

12. *The Karate Kid* (Los Angeles, CA: Columbia Pictures, 2010).

13. This insight comes from Marcus Warner and Jim Wilder, *Rare Leadership: 4 Uncommon Habits for Increasing Trust, Joy, and Engagement in the People You Lead* (Chicago: Moody, 2016).

14. See 1 Thessalonians 5:5.
15. Luke 18:1, NLT.

CHAPTER 8: FAITH AND VODKA

1. Matthew 26:41.
2. Romans 7:15-21, MSG.
3. Romans 7:25, MSG.
4. Psalm 119:1, MSG.
5. See James 1:17.
6. *Rocky Balboa* (Beverly Hills, CA: Metro-Goldwyn-Mayer, 2006).
7. See Romans 8:28.
8. C. S. Lewis, *A Grief Observed* (Greenwich, CT: Seabury Press, 1961), 7.

CHAPTER 9: IRREPRESSIBLE

1. Congratulations to those of you who know that James Cameron didn't write *Blade Runner*.
2. See John 10:10.
3. John 15:11-12.
4. See Psalm 16:11, ESV.
5. See Jeremiah 29:13.
6. 2 Corinthians 12:2-4.
7. *The Handmaid's Tale*, "Offred," season 1, episode 1 (Hulu, aired on April 26, 2017).
8. Revelation 3:20-21, ESV.
9. See Hebrews 11:6.
10. John 15:4-11, ESV.
11. See John 8:31-32.
12. *Heidi* (Burbank, CA: Disney Channel, 1993).
13. Philippians 4:6-9, MSG.
14. See Romans 8:31-39.

THE NAVIGATORS® STORY

THANK YOU for picking up this NavPress book! We hope it has been a blessing to you.

NavPress is a ministry of The Navigators. The Navigators began in the 1930s, when a young California lumberyard worker named Dawson Trotman was impacted by basic discipleship principles and felt called to teach those principles to others. He saw this mission as an echo of 2 Timothy 2:2: "And the things you have heard me say in the presence of many witnesses entrust to reliable people who will also be qualified to teach others" (NIV).

In 1933, Trotman and his friends began discipling members of the US Navy. By the end of World War II, thousands of men on ships and bases around the world were learning the principles of spiritual multiplication by the intentional, person-to-person teaching of God's Word.

After World War II, The Navigators expanded its relational ministry to include college campuses; local churches; the Glen Eyrie Conference Center and Eagle Lake Camps in Colorado Springs, Colorado; and neighborhood and citywide initiatives across the country and around the world.

Today, with more than 2,600 US staff members—and local ministries in more than 100 countries—The Navigators continues the transformational process of making disciples who make more disciples, advancing the Kingdom of God in a world that desperately needs the hope and salvation of Jesus Christ and the encouragement to grow deeper in relationship with Him.

NAVPRESS was created in 1975 to advance the calling of The Navigators by bringing biblically rooted and culturally relevant products to people who want to know and love Christ more deeply. In January 2014, NavPress entered an alliance with Tyndale House Publishers to strengthen and better position our rich content for the future. Through *THE MESSAGE* Bible and other resources, NavPress seeks to bring positive spiritual movement to people's lives.

If you're interested in learning more or becoming involved with The Navigators, go to navigators.org. For more discipleship content from The Navigators and NavPress authors, visit thedisciplemaker.org. May God bless you in your walk with Him!